I'M DONE WITH EITHER/OR THINKING

ERICA RENÉE

Printed in the United States of America.

First printing, 2017

ISBN-13: 978-0-9996049-0-8

www.EricaRenee.co

What People Are Saying About *I'm Done With Either/Or Thinking* . . .

"Our dear friend, Minister Erica Moore has written an important and powerful book that is a gift of God for this generation. With an eloquent delivery she beautifully shares with us her incredible journey of transformation and freedom from the bondage and burden that all of us face in our lives: wrong thinking. This book is not just a blessing, it's a key in your life to breakthrough the limitations that have confined, controlled, and crippled your life from being all that God wants it to be! As she states: "It's hard to serve a limitless God, when we have limited thinking."

Dr. Michael Maiden,
Founder & Pastor of Church For The Nations

"This book is an invitation to align your life with heaven! I read Erica's new book with great anticipation, knowing that I would be encouraged, but I found so much more. In *I'm Done With Either/Or Thinking* she shares hard earned wisdom that is made easily accessible and can be practically applied. Consider the dream of thinking God's thoughts where heaven becomes our natural instinct and there are no limitations of choosing Either/Or. I highly recommend this engaging resource to anyone who truly desires to embrace the richness of God's design that is available to each one of us . . . get caught up in the dream and begin living your limitless heritage as a child of the King!"

Audrey Meisner
Bestselling Author, Marriage Under Cover
Co-Founder, Love Married Life ®

"This is a powerful book revealing that you have choices to make and that our choices will determine what life we will live. God has planned to give you the best life ever, and we can choose His destiny for us daily in every area or we can choose to run our own life and do it our way. We have freedom of choice, but we are responsible for our own choice in life. This thought-provoking book will help you to understand that God is bigger than your biggest dreams and does far above what you expect or imagine. God is limitless in your life! You will be blessed beyond words in reading this book."

Dr. Tom and Maureen Anderson,
Living Word Bible Church Founders

Table of Contents

Dedication

I dedicate this book to my amazing mom that I miss more than I thought humanly possible. I watched her slip away on October 6, 2016. Although she knew it would happen one day, she did not get the opportunity to see me become an author. When she was naming me in the hospital, the thought came to her, "Erica Renée would be a great name when she is an author." And so it was the name placed on my birth certificate. This is why instead of using my last name, I have chosen to be known to my literary audience by my first and middle.

I will dedicate every book to you because you dedicated your life to me. I love you more than words can express. I am the woman I am today because of you and I will always be grateful for your self-sacrificing love and friendship. If I am half the woman you were, I will have accomplished something great. I look forward to seeing you again. Bye for now.

Acknowledgments

I want to acknowledge my wonderful husband, Sean R. Moore, who is such a steady, solid example of what it means to be a Godly leader. I have learned so much from you. Thank you for all of the years that you have poured life into me.

My amazing team of ladies: Nadia Brown, Elaine Cauley, Isha Cogborn, Monica Debro, Yubeka Riddick, and Kendra Tillman, who helped to coach, encourage, and assist me in completing this project. I can never thank you enough for being my life vest and cheering squad when I needed it.

My awesome book editor, Latoya Rosario, for all the late night sessions.

My book cover art designer, Rey Contreras Jr., for his meticulous eye for detail and passion for excellence.

My best friend, Min. Oshea Vega, for being the voice of wisdom through the storms of life and the fun voice of escape on the other end of the phone.

My church family for giving me time, space, and interactions necessary to develop into someone you'd want to follow and for being so supportive along the way.

My children, Heaven, Sean, Isaiah, and Hannah for giving me four beautiful reasons for waking up in the morning.

My God who is my everything.

Introduction

It was a Friday night in Phoenix, Arizona, and more than 100 women had gathered for a women's ministry event at my church. I watched as they played the "Would You Rather?" icebreaker game. The ladies were giggling and shouting loudly over the thumping background music. I almost had it turned down, but decided not to since it added to the excitement of the already interesting game. Some of the women looked perplexed as they asked people they had never spoken to silly questions, such as "Would you rather go on a date with bad breath or body odor?" or "Would you rather live as a dog or live as a cat?" Some questions were more serious such as, "Would you rather love and not be loved back, or be loved, but never love?" Or "Would you rather invent the cure for cancer or a cure for AIDS?" As the game progressed, I noticed many women began to wonder why we were playing such a game, especially in a church environment. What does this have to do with the gospel of Jesus Christ? When one of the ladies on my leadership team suggested we do this icebreaker, I initially thought the same thing: "What does this have to do with anything? What is the purpose for this exercise?"

And then, it hit me. Certainly questions such as "Would you rather be hairy all over or completely bald?" seem silly and we dismiss them right away by thinking, "Neither! I'd rather have hair where I'm supposed to have hair and no hair where I don't want it." But isn't this the game we play in our minds on a daily basis? It's the "Would-You-Rather" game. It can sound like the following:

- Would you rather have a faithful spouse and no passion in your marriage, or never commit to anyone and live it up when you're young, but be lonely when you're older?

- Would you rather be a stay-at-home mom and enjoy watching your kids grow at the expense of your career goals, or pursue your career at the expense of having a close-knit family?

- Would you rather treat yourself to what you deserve by eating whatever you want whenever you want at the expense of your health, or live a disciplined life where you don't enjoy your food or social gatherings, but you're really healthy and have a nice body?

Sure, we've all played the "Would-You-Rather" game at least once, and many of us do it multiple times a day. Sometimes the questions are silly and meaningless, but at other times, the answers we give could change the very course of our lives and drastically affect the destiny of others.

The statements listed above are examples of what I call **Either/Or** Thoughts. These thoughts come for the purpose of distracting us from the target we should aim our lives towards, which is God and His purposes. The sneaky thing about **Either/Or** thoughts is that they often sound like our own thoughts or even God's thoughts. Sometimes they come from suggestions made by our loved ones. As a result, we tend to embrace the thoughts, not realizing that their purpose in our lives is to steal, kill, and destroy the best life God has for us.

The thief's purpose is to steal and kill and destroy. My purpose is to give them a rich and satisfying life.
(John. 10:10 NLT)

So in this book, we will define what **Either/Or** thoughts are, learn how to identify where they come from, become empowered to get rid of them, and recognize what thoughts to replace them with so that nothing will prevent us from properly serving and representing our limitless God. And while I know you may want to skip some chapters to go to the ones you feel best connect with where you are in your life right now, I encourage you to read them in sequential order. I believe the foundation laid within the first few chapters will help you to better understand and appropriate the tools revealed in the later chapters.

Chapter 1 | What Is An **Either/Or** Thought?

I'll never forget the day, a sincere, Christian had a heart-to-heart conversation with me concerning some of the details I had revealed about my ministerial call and family life. This person in so many words basically said that there was no possible way that I could be a good wife at home, minister as a pastor's wife for the church, be a mom to my children, and pursue the career and ministerial dreams I had in my heart. She asserted that I would lose my relationship with my children or that they would go wayward. Or that I'd lose my marriage while in hot pursuit of my call or some combination of both. Her assumptions hit the core of the **Either/Or** thoughts I had been wrestling with for years.

As a child, I felt strongly that I was supposed to marry a pastor and was confident that I would have four children. As I got older, my call to do many things at once in the home, in ministry, and in business became more and more evident. I had many conversations with God concerning my inability to accomplish everything well and at a high level.

My **Either/Or** Thought: "I can **Either** be a good wife and mother and stay at home, **Or** I can excel in ministry and business opportunities, but I cannot do all successfully at the same time."

And this was not the only **Either/Or** Thought that I had. The reality is that now I realize that I have dealt with limited thinking for most of my life and it has greatly impacted my ability to become the person I know I have the potential of being. The hard truth is that it took me about nine years to complete this book because while I was trying to encourage you to get rid of your **Either/Or** mindsets, I was struggling with several of my own.

It is my sincere hope that my transparency and wisdom that I have gained through God's Word and through personal experience will assist you in identifying your own **Either/Or** thoughts and dismantle them for good.

An **Either/Or Thought** or **Either/Or Thinking** is designed to place limitations on what we think God, others, and even we ourselves can do, receive, and achieve. This thought follows the premise that in order for one area of our lives to flourish, another area must suffer. It's thinking that we simply can't accomplish more than one desire at the same time.

If we allow these thoughts to take residence in our minds long enough and form firm conclusions concerning certain subjects, a stronghold may form. A **stronghold** is a fortified castle of thoughts or arguments that we hold safely and protect in our minds. The only thing that can destroy a stronghold is the Word of God.

These **Either/Or** thoughts or strongholds might have been planted in our minds years ago possibly when we were children. Many times, we don't even know that the thoughts are there until God challenges us to do a particular task, or to remove a habit or person from our lives. Suddenly, we are bombarded from within with all of the reasons why we couldn't possibly carry out His request. Even the heroes of faith dealt with this issue. Take Moses, for example:

God's proposition: *"Come now, therefore, and I will send you to Pharaoh, that you may bring My people, the children of Israel, out of Egypt." (Ex. 3:10)*

Moses' Rebuttal 1: *"But Moses said to God, Who am I, that I should go to Pharaoh, and that I should bring the children of Israel out of Egypt?" (Ex. 3:11)*

Either/Or Thought Translation: I am not qualified to go before Pharaoh. You **Either** have to be a king **Or** a general to be taken seriously by this man, and I'm neither, so I don't qualify.

How many times have you done this—limited what God could do in you and through you based on your own estimation of yourself or of others? I've done it too many times to count. I will make this statement now, and I'm sure you'll hear it throughout the book, because it bears repeating:

"It's hard to serve the limitless God when we have limited thinking."

This is why we're attacking this issue. For too long, the enemy of our souls has been neutralizing our potency and effectiveness in carrying out God's orders due to our own inability to recognize and dismantle his assaults. The **Either/Or** thoughts come to our minds, and today, we have to decide not to guard or protect them or allow them to form castles within us any longer. It is our responsibility to cast down the imaginations—collections of images—that create inward pictures contrary to God's will for our lives (2 Cor. 10:5). It would be nice if God would zap them for us, but it doesn't work that way. The responsibility is ours, and we are capable of doing it by the grace of God and with the help of Holy Spirit.

Quick Review

Either/Or Thinking is characterized by believing that in order for one area of my life to flourish, another area must suffer. A person with this mindset has difficulty believing that she can successfully achieve both at the same time, so she thinks she has to choose. This causes us to focus on one area, while neglecting the other.

Here are some examples of **Either/Or** thoughts:

- I can **Either** put in long hours at my job, and be successful, **Or** I can spend more time with my child and be a good parent.

- I can **Either** have a great social life **Or** focus on my relationship with God.

- I can **Either** be a bored, secure employee, **Or** I can be a happy, broke artist.

- I can **Either** accept the (man/woman) interested in me now, **Or** I can wait and possibly never have an intimate relationship, because there may not be a better option out there.

These were some of the statements members from my church submitted to me when I asked them to share their biggest **Either/Or** thoughts. If we don't attack thinking like this head on, they could form strongholds that could remain for years. These thoughts contradict the edifying statements God says in the Bible concerning us:

- I can do all things through Christ who strengthens me. (Phil. 4:13)

- Delight yourself also in the LORD, and He shall give you the desires of your heart. (Ps. 37:4)

- Trust in the LORD with all your heart; and lean not on your own understanding; in all thy ways acknowledge Him, and He shall direct your paths. (Prov. 3:5–6)

- But seek first the kingdom of God, and His righteousness; and all these things shall be added to you. (Matt. 6:33)

- Beloved, I pray that you may prosper in all things and be in health, even as your soul prospers. (3 John 1:2)

- Now to Him Who, by (in consequence of) the [action of His] power that is at work within us, is able to [carry out His purpose and] do superabundantly, far over and above all that we [dare] ask or think [infinitely beyond our highest prayers, desires, thoughts, hopes, or dreams]. (Eph. 3:20 AMP)

- The thief's purpose is to steal, kill and destroy. My purpose is to give life in all its fullness. (John 10:10 TLB)

9

Jesus came to give us His John 10:10 life—abundant, satisfied, fulfilled living, not the tired, miserable, barely getting by way of living. If that's what He came to give, then let's get aggressive and take what rightfully belongs to us as heirs of the kingdom of God! The word "life" in John 10:10 translates as the Greek word Zoë, and it means the God-kind of life.

In other words, Jesus was saying that He came, not just to save us from sin and it's penalty (and thank God He did do that), but to also give us the kind of life God would have if He were you or me. Now, let's ponder that for a moment. If God were you, would He be wrestling with an **Either/Or** thought? Would He have had this thought: "I can **Either** save the human race **Or** regret creating mankind and wipe it out?" Of course not! NO! He thought then and still thinks, "All things are possible to him that believes!" (Mark 9:23)

So see, it is vitally important that as we endeavor to live our best lives now—the Zoë life—that we rid ourselves of these defeated mindsets that obviously don't come from God. They come from the thief—Satan—whose mission is to steal from us, kill our dreams, and destroy whatever life God would have us live. The good news is that according to scripture, we've already won this battle:

And they overcame him by the blood of the Lamb, and by the word of their testimony. (Revelation 12:11a)

We have already overcome! We simply have to walk it out and together, and through this book, we'll find out how.

10

Chapter 2 | Where Do **Either/Or** Thoughts Come From?

As stated previously, God is not the source of **Either/Or** thinking. Limiting thoughts totally contradict His Word and embracing thoughts of limitation make it virtually impossible to please God or to fully carry out His instructions to us.

But without faith it is impossible to please Him: for he that comes to God must believe that He is, and that He is a rewarder of those who diligently seek him. (Hebrews 11:6)

All **Either/Or** thoughts are fear based. They don't originate from faith, so they can't come from God Almighty, the Lord of faith, love, and hope.

So, if God is not the source, who is? Is it we ourselves? While it is our responsibility to prevent our thoughts from becoming a jumbled mess inside of our minds—preventing us from accomplishing anything of substance in this life—it is highly unlikely that we are purposefully sabotaging ourselves every day with limiting thoughts. So that eliminates us. That only leaves one person—Satan. He's the god of fear, so of course, he'd attack us with fearful, limited thinking for the purpose of getting us to doubt our God-given identity and take on the counterfeit identity he and society offers us.

Now, in today's world our society doesn't like acknowledging his existence. It's seen as an archaic way of thinking to even admit that he is at work in our modern world. But if you surf the Web, turn on the news, or step outside and look around for a minute, it is obvious that Satan, the god of this world, is still at work. And what is he doing? Fiddling with people's minds.

The Ruler of this world has blinded the minds of those who don't believe. They cannot see the light of the Good News— the message about the divine greatness of Christ.
(2 Corinthians 4:4a ERV)

Now, of course, this scripture is referring to people who have not yet received Jesus as their Lord and Savior, but the gospel is more inclusive than only a salvation prayer. If we as believers in Christ doubt the principles of God's Word, then we'll be like other people who haven't even received salvation through Jesus yet. We'll live beneath our privileges and rights as heirs of God and joint heirs with Christ and wind up settling for the status quo life instead of the Zoë life.

I believe you're reading this book because you sense that there is more to life than struggling through and taking it one day at a time. You believe that God has a plan for you, and you're not going to settle for some second rate plan. Instead, you'll take your rightful place, because you know God wills it, you are worth it, and people need you.

Either/Or Thinking Produces Either/Or Living

When we get rid of the wrong thinking, we can enjoy the right kind of living. People will benefit, and God will be glorified in seeing His word fulfilled in and through you. Bro. Kenneth Hagin said, "(Negative) thoughts are like birds. You can't keep them from flying around your head, but you can prevent them from building nests in your hair." It is our responsibility to sift through our thoughts and eliminate the ones that are not supported by God's Word. It would be nice if God would do it for us, but that's not how it works. This means that we must first know what God's Word says. In order for this to happen, we cannot be a people who simply let our Bible's collect dust and attend church when convenient. We must be students of the Scriptures in the same manner of Jesus' original disciples. They were disciplined ones: Students who regularly spent time mastering their subject— the Word of God. This is vitally important, because Satan knows the Word, too, although, he himself doesn't live by it. Contrarily, he will twist the truths of the Bible in an attempt to get us to err.

One of the main reasons Satan comes to our minds with the wrong thoughts is to challenge our identity in God. As soon as Jesus' identity was confirmed by the voice of God from Heaven, the Holy Spirit descended, and John the Baptist testified that Jesus was indeed the Messiah (Luke 4:1–2), Satan immediately began tempting Jesus. Why? To get Him to doubt what God had said about Him and to pressure Him to "prove" who He was instead of simply "being" who He was. Satan does this to us, too.

We finally receive a revelation of what our purpose is and then he attempts to get us to compete with others or to battle internally within ourselves concerning if we've got what it takes to bring it into fruition. Some of us battle with whether or not we even deserve to have been given the assignment. However, Jesus had confidence in who He was (probably from all of those years finding Himself in the book Isaiah). Jesus' knowledge and understanding of the scriptures prevented Him from taking the bait He was being offered, which would have caused Him to forfeit what belonged to Him.

Jesus' water baptism and wilderness temptation found in Mark 1:9–13 describes an experience that deserves our attention. Jesus was driven or led into the wilderness by the Holy Spirit to be tempted and harassed in His mind by the evil one for 40 days! Having to resist the devil in the wilderness is not the same as baking cookies. It's a mental workout. Nevertheless, God must have decided it was necessary for Jesus' development.

I don't know about you, but I would much rather go through life letting my Shepherd lead me in green pastures and besides still waters (Ps. 23). I don't want Holy Spirit to lead me into a dry, deserted place void of food and water only to be annoyed relentlessly by an enemy whose goal is to kill me, steal from me, and to destroy me (John 10:10). I would much rather eat whatever I want and still have washboard abs because I blessed the food before I ate it. I would rather skip the physical exercise necessary to keep my skin from becoming flabby as I age and just naturally keep the elasticity given to us at birth. Wouldn't you rather study the Bible for 10 minutes instead of studying it for years and still pass the most challenging life test ever? Of course you would! I would too!

But our Savior, our greatest human example on how to live for God in an imperfect world faced immense difficulties immediately after attempting to walk in His purpose. We need to understand that challenge doesn't mean that we are not in the will

14

of God or that we have somehow missed Holy Spirit's leading. On the contrary, the hardship might actually confirm that we are on the right track. Resist the urge to relieve the pressure. We must develop the skill of dominating in our minds if we expect to have the productivity Jesus experienced in His life.

Now, it's important to note that although Holy Spirit did the leading, He did not do the tempting. The devil did that. And what was his strategy? Satan . . .

- Attempted to examine Jesus to analyze whether or not Jesus believed the Word of God like He said He did

- Trash-talked Jesus to the degree that He felt compelled to prove who He was

- Desired to entice Jesus to deviate from God's plan and take a shortcut to achieve desired results

Satan's tactics are still the same, and we can learn how to properly resist his temptation by observing how Jesus responded when he was tempted. God does not need to tempt us. He already knows what we believe. He knows who we are better than we know ourselves, and He would never tempt us to sin, because the wages of sin is death (James 1:13). Remember, Jesus came to give us life (Rom. 6:23, John 10:10).

This epic temptation story is detailed in the first three gospels. When you can, I encourage you to read the entire historical account in Matthew 4:2–11. Phrases are used to describe Satan's invitations as if he were taking Jesus on a trip. For example, v. 5

15

says, "Then, the devil took Him up into the holy city, set Him on the pinnacle of the temple, and tempted Jesus to jump off the edge.

Let me be clear: Satan did not take Jesus by the hand and physically move Him to the top of the temple. If you were Jesus, would you take Satan's hand and follow him anywhere? Of course not! So how did Satan "take" Jesus to the pinnacle of the temple? The same way he takes us places—through thoughts and imaginations. I believe Jesus was in the wilderness, possibly on the top of a mountain or large hill, and He visualized the top of the temple. Then, Satan spoke a suicidal thought to Him, "Why not just jump off? God loves you; He'll save you." And in the same breath of making such a ridiculous offer, he quotes scripture:

He said to Jesus, 'If you are the Son of God, jump off, because the Scriptures say, 'God will command his angels to help you, and their hands will catch you, so that you will not hit your foot on a rock. (Matthew 4:6 ERV)

Satan is a master tempter who will use the Word of God to his advantage against us if we don't rightly discern the truths the Bible holds. This same Bible that has brought liberation and freedom to so many was also used out of context to justify slavery in the early years of America's history. The truth of the glorious Gospel can be twisted to satisfy the needs and desires of those with the wrong motives. It can be misunderstood by well-meaning people who misappropriate certain principles. Thankfully, there are great resources available to assist you in your studies to properly understand the truths this God-breathed book provides to those who put their trust in Him.

Jesus' trust was in God His Father. His Father had confirmed who He was and how pleased He was with Him. Perhaps you can relate. Maybe you've had an encounter with God at a service or in your own personal time with Him. God revealed some truth to you or revealed more concerning your assignment in life. You felt enlightened and privileged to receive the revelation and immediately, here come the **Either/Or** thoughts:

> **Either/Or Thought:** "You can't do that, you're not old enough or experienced enough."

> **Translation:** "You **Either** wait until you have some experience, **Or** you can't do what God called you to do."

> **Either/Or Thought:** "You can't do that; you remember your past."

> **Translation:** "You **Either** stay in your lane and do what you're worthy to do based on your past mistakes, **Or** you'll get out there in the industry you endeavor to tap into, and it will eat you alive."

I dealt with thoughts such as these when God spoke to me in 2008 and told me that He put me on the Earth to write. I had been eagerly pursuing clarity regarding my purpose for years and now He had finally explained my life's purpose in two sentences: "I put you on the Earth to write. You will speak the truth in love with much conviction." I was overwhelmed with gratitude of having heard from the Creator of the universe. How majestic and mighty He is, but oh, how thoughtful and loving of Him to speak to me in such a manner that makes me feel like I'm the only child he has and that nothing else is as important to Him than getting a message to me! While writing feverishly in my journal and basking in the moment, they came—those doubtful questioning words . . .

Write?

Write to whom?

Write about what?

How?

How much is this going to cost?

You are a stay-at-home mom with a 1-year-old baby and another one on the way—this is ridiculous!

Who is going to watch your kids while you write?

You are an unknown.

Who will even buy your book?

I wish I could say I had the courage of Jesus to immediately slay these thoughts with the Word but I did not. I did manage to muster up enough boldness to share the revelation with my husband the same night I got it. But I did not start typing a single word or even try to do so until over a year later. I was in an internal mental battle over my ability to carry out the task at hand. How ironic that the first book God told me to write was on the mind. I would have preferred to write about something a little more cozy and comfortable to my internal reality. I didn't want to have to admit my own **Either/Or** thought drama occurring daily.

But of course, God is into the win-win result. If my transparency and humility leads you on a healthy journey of self-discovery that develops mature, solid, pure thinking that results in the improvement of your everyday life, then my nine-year mental war was worth it. You are worth it.

The tempting statements that Satan said to Jesus in Matthew 4 were all **Either/Or** thoughts. Let me show you:

- The devil came to tempt him and said, 'If you are the Son of God, tell these rocks to become bread.' (Matt. 4:3 ERV)

- **Translation**: "**Either** you're the Son of God and you have the power to turn these stones into bread, **Or** you're not really the Son of God and won't be able to do it."

Thankfully, Jesus was secure in His identity and responded by quoting a scripture found in Deuteronomy 8:3:

But Jesus told him, 'No! The Scriptures say, 'People do not live by bread alone, but by every word that comes from the mouth of God.' (Matthew 4:4 NLT)

Responding with the Word when our imaginations are creating motion pictures that resemble horror movies instead of light comedies is essential. God gave us our imaginations to assist us in dreaming big dreams and using our faith to carry out His will and purpose. He did not give them to us so we could torture ourselves by allowing renegade thoughts to permeate our minds with what-if syndrome and should've-would've-could've disease.

REVELATION: EVERY THOUGHT DOESN'T COME FROM GOD AND EVERY THOUGHT DOESN'T COME FROM YOU.

So resist the urge to beat yourself up and feel like a horrible excuse for a Christian if a less than holy, fear-filled thought crosses your mind.

Satan tempted Jesus at least three times. Perhaps it was more than that but these were the three attempts that were recorded. Many times Christians become dismayed when they are bombarded with mental attacks as if it's out of the ordinary for these things to happen. But that is not the case.

Dear friends, don't be surprised at the fiery trials you are going through, as if something strange were happening to you.
(1 Peter 5:7)

We must remember: If Satan came hard after Jesus' mind in a solitary and desolate place when He was physically weak and hungry, he will come hard after us when we find ourselves famished in life and in a dry place as well. This is why we must avoid unnecessarily isolating ourselves. Instead, we should stay connected to the body of Christ.

When police respond to a threat, they don't go alone; they have a partner with them. If the situation is dangerous enough, they'll send out a page requesting additional back up. We must do the same. When situations get tough, it's not the time to hide in a corner and try to handle problems on our own. It's time to convene with our own company who can rally around us so we don't have

20

to fight alone. Also, they can remind us of what God's Word does say. However, in Jesus' case, He was alone, and Satan made Jesus an offer that he still makes to people today.

- Next the devil took him to the peak of a very high mountain and showed him all the kingdoms of the world and their glory. 'I will give it all to you,' he said, 'if you will kneel down and worship me.' (Matt. 4:8–9 NLT)

- **Translation**: You can **Either** do this God's way and miss out on all that the world has to offer, **Or** you can take a shorter route, cut corners, follow my lead, ignore God's commandment, and you'll achieve success in life a whole lot faster.

Repeatedly, Satan used Jesus' imagination against Him. As Jesus imagined all of the splendor, magnificence, preeminence, and excellence of the kingdoms of the world, Satan inserted a thought: "You can have all of this now, if. . ." Unfortunately, when he makes such offers to mankind, he never shares the catch: "But you'll lose everything else in the process." Jesus didn't fall for this trap. Instead he referenced the scripture found in Deut. 6:13 saying that we should only worship and serve the Lord God.

It's important to note that Jesus, while perfect still had imperfect thoughts. However, Jesus was already prepared to face the mind-game Satan presented. He didn't have to call the church for counseling, didn't have to try to look up a scripture on a Bible app, and didn't have to fumble through the channels of His television for a Christian program. There is nothing wrong with any of these things. But given the circumstance, these tools might not be accessible to us when we need them. We have to hide God's Word securely in our hearts (Ps. 119:11).

> When we find our imaginations running wild down the hill toward Hell instead of upwards toward Heaven, we need to lasso them with the Word of God and bring them back to the center of balance.

So what happened after Jesus victoriously prevented Satan from giving Him a nervous breakdown and playing hopscotch with the thoughts in His head?

And when the devil had ended every [the complete cycle of] temptation, he [temporarily] left Him [that is, stood off from Him] until another more opportune and favorable time. Then Jesus went back full of and under the power of the [Holy] Spirit into Galilee, and the fame of Him spread through the whole region round about. And He Himself conducted [a course of] teaching in their synagogues, being recognized and honored and praised by all.
(Luke 4:13–15 AMP)

The Holy Spirit had already descended on Jesus, but the power didn't come until He resisted the devil and put Him on the run (James 4:7). He won what Joyce Meyer calls, "the battlefield of the mind," and the cowardly devil ran. He'll run from us too when we make it obvious during his litmus test of temptation that we know who we are and whose we are. Also, notice that the fame Satan promised to Jesus, if He lowered His standards and lived life backwards from what He knew was right, came anyway. Jesus was honored and praised by all simply by getting in His lane and obeying God in what He was called to do during His life. I've

22

heard it said that God doesn't pay up every Friday, but when He does, boy, oh boy, does He pay! As an added bonus, the blessing of the Lord doesn't come with a catch, strings attached, or an unforeseen penalty.

Having overcome the devil's temptations, Jesus stepped out into His ministerial assignment full of the Holy Ghost and power! Because He didn't become insecure from the thoughts Satan threw at Him, He confidently marched into the temple and proclaimed who He was. No identity crisis here! In life, others may not agree with who you say you are, but if your testimony of yourself agrees with that of God's testimony of you, then you don't need anything more!

Now, Satan left Jesus, but returned when he deemed it to be a more favorable time (Luke 4:13). This is where we usually get confused. We feel like we won a battle and should never have to fight another one ever again. However, it simply doesn't work that way.

Stay alert! Watch out for your great enemy, the devil. He prowls around like a roaring lion, looking for someone to devour.
(1 Peter 5:8 NLT)

Satan doesn't disappear off of the face of the earth because we quoted a few scriptures and didn't have a pity party when things didn't go our way. No, the devil waits until he thinks our guard is down, and he strikes again, usually through our thought life or through opposition from other people. Let's wise up and stay prepared in the realm of the Spirit to win every battle like Jesus did.

Chapter 3: When Do **Either/Or** Thoughts Show Up?

Remember, all **Either/Or** thoughts are fear based and sent by the god of fear to cause us to doubt who we are in Christ. It is a direct attack on our identity. These thoughts can show up at various times throughout our lives. I will use Biblical examples to describe life situations and circumstances in which **Either/Or** thoughts rear their ugly heads. Sadly, one of the **places Either/Or** thoughts appear is within a family:

❖ Sometimes, Either/Or thoughts are passed down from generation to generation by tradition or words that are constantly spoken to us as children.

Take Gideon, for example. When the angel appeared and called him a "mighty man of valor," Gideon told the angel, "I am the least in my Father's house" (Judg. 6:15). Well, I'm sure he wasn't born thinking that way. Babies come into the world not knowing anything about limitations. Watch a child long enough, and you'll laugh at the things they try to do. They try to fly, transform into race cars, and become princesses without plastic surgery or a magic potion. They can be so bold and daring in their actions that they have to be told repeatedly, "Be careful!"

Over time, a child learns fear, lack, doubt, unbelief, and limitation. I'm convinced Gideon didn't come up with the thought of being "the least in his father's house" on his own. Without a doubt someone—we do not know who—told him that statement on a repeated basis. Perhaps the societal norms of the time told him nonverbally that he should stay in his place and his place was at the bottom. We don't know exactly how he developed this mentality but I am confident that it did not come from God.

Adam and Eve had a similar experience. When the two sinned in the Garden of Eden, Adam and Eve hid from God. Adam told God he hid because he knew he was naked and became afraid. God asked, "Who told you that you were naked?" (Gen. 3:9–11) And that's the question I have for you: Who told you . . .

- ". . . you're not smart enough"

- ". . . you're not pretty enough"

- ". . . you're not strong enough"

- ". . . you're not rich enough"

- ". . . you're too young"

- ". . . you're too old"

- ". . . you're too dark"

- ". . . you're too pale"

- ". . . you're too fat"

- ". . . you're too skinny"

- ". . . women can't do that"

- ". . . men don't do that"

- ". . . your past has disqualified you"

- ". . . you're the least likely to succeed"

Who Told You These Things?

For sure, it wasn't God. So you don't have to receive them as being true! Instead, reject them as being lies. Gideon said that He was the least in his father's house because that is how he viewed his status in life. Perhaps some "loving" family member pointed this out to him. But Jesus said,

In my Father's house are many mansions: if it were not so,
I would have told you. I go to prepare a place for you.
(John 14:2)

It doesn't sound like Jesus viewed Gideon as being the least in His Heavenly Father's house, now does it? Remember, man's opinion of you should never shape or distort your opinion of yourself. Let's allow the Word of God to determine for us who we are and what we are here to do. Let the words of the Father qualify, edify, and equip you.

Since he did not spare even his own Son but gave him up
for us all, won't he also give us everything else?
(Romans 8:32 NLT)

This scripture brings up a good point. If God thought we were priceless enough to ransom us back to Himself by offering up His Son, then that means we're pretty expensive and valuable. Now, if God Almighty, the Creator and Sustainer of the universe and everything in it thinks we're that special, who are we not to agree with Him? God is not the one whispering those self–defeating thoughts listed above into our ears. That's the devil's job, and it's time we hand him a pink slip and let him know his position in our lives has been terminated. It's important for us to remember who has been the originator of these thoughts. It has been Satan.

Even if the person he used was our grandparent, parent, sibling, neighbor, teacher, co-worker, or friend, the source was Satan. If we don't recognize this, we could spend a lifetime angry and bitter toward the people he influenced to say those rotten things to us. Then, unforgiveness gets in our hearts and that is something none of us can afford to embrace.

The word forgive in the Hebrew and Greek Strong's Concordance Dictionary usually means to "send away." We need to actively "send away" those negative emotions attached to the memories of what happened to us or didn't happen for us in our past. When we realize who our real enemy is, we can release those people who hurt us and not allow their error to paralyze our present or dictate our future. Instead, we can press aggressively forward into what God has for us.

I believe societal norms of class and the economy may have led Gideon to view himself the wrong way. And cultural norms can have the same impact on our lives today.

❖ Sometimes we develop **Either/Or** thoughts because of our culture and the environment we have been exposed to. These societal norms may have been created through various avenues such as media, entertainment, and education.

For example, here in America, entire groups of people are bombarded with **Either/Or** thoughts:

28

- Singles are sent the **Either/Or** message: "You can **Either** be single and free, **Or** be married and live in bondage."

- Women are sent the message: "You can **Either** concentrate on your family **Or** your career, but you can't focus on both and excel in both areas simultaneously."

- Men are sent the message: "You are **Either** a real man with a bustling career, the latest gadgets, the most luxurious cars, and more than one woman, **Or** you're living beneath your privilege."

It's important for believers to remember that we are in the world, but told to not be of the world (John 17:16).

Do not love this world nor the things it offers you, for when you love the world, you do not have the love of the Father in you. (1 John 2:15 NLT)

You [are like] unfaithful wives [having illicit love affairs with the world and breaking your marriage vow to God]! Do you not know that being the world's friend is being God's enemy? So whoever chooses to be a friend of the world takes his stand as an enemy of God. (James 4:4 AMP)

In 2 Corinthians 5:20, Paul referred to believers as ambassadors of Christ pleading with others to be reconciled unto God. We must remember that as Christians, our No. 1 responsibility in life is to REPresent God's Kingdom—not the culture in which we live or into which we were born. Foreign ambassadors are sent to other countries to represent where they are originally from and to do business for the king, president, or diplomat who sent them. They do not adapt to the culture of the foreign country. This same principle applies to us, because God, our King, chose us.

For you are a chosen people. You are royal priests, a holy nation, God's very own possession. As a result, you can show others the goodness of God, for he called you out of the darkness into his wonderful light. Once you had no identity as a people; now you are God's people. Once you received no mercy; now you have received God's mercy. Dear friends, I warn you as 'temporary residents and foreigners' to keep away from worldly desires that wage war against your very souls. (1 Peter 2: 9–11 NLT)

Even the men and women we admire in the Bible understood that we are from another place: Heaven. They did not entangle themselves with the affairs of the world, but sought to please the one Who had sent them to the world on an assignment (Heb. 11:13–16 AMP). Timothy reminded us that we are in a literal spiritual war and are solders of the Most High God warring against the forces of darkness. In war, soldiers can't get so consumed with their personal lives that they forget to defend themselves against enemy fire. Soldiers have to be sober and vigilant, and they need to take out their enemy before the enemy attacks them (1 Pet. 5:8).

Endure suffering along with me, as a good soldier of Christ Jesus. Soldiers don't get tied up in the affairs of civilian life, for then they cannot please the officer who enlisted them. (2 Timothy 2:3–4 NLT)

We are here on a heavenly assignment, and it's important that we do our job and not get so engrossed in societal norms and popular culture that we forget that we even have an assignment. It doesn't really matter what types of **Either/Or** messages our society sends our way. If we remember that we are only pilgrims and strangers in this land sent on a heavenly assignment by our King and commander in chief, we'll know that those limitations don't apply to us.

The next vehicle through which Either/Or thoughts might develop occurs when we experience unfortunate life events.

❖ Sometimes we receive **Either/Or** thoughts because of trauma, affliction, or persecution.

Tamar, King David's daughter, is an example of this. She was raped by her brother, Amnon, and never recovered from the horrific experience. 2 Samuel 13 reveals Tamar's story, but I will paraphrase it for you.

A man was obsessed with his half-sister so severely that he lured her into his bedroom and raped her. She begged him to stop; she even begged him to marry her first. And in those days and in that culture, this would have been permissible. But no matter how much she pleaded, he did not listen. He had his way with her and to her surprise, turned on her immediately. He became enraged and forced her out of his room, never speaking to her again. Her other brother, Absalom, found out about it and advised her not to talk about it. He moved her into his place, and she was never vindicated. She didn't receive counseling. Her father, who was the king and could have done something, but didn't. Her violator was never sentenced or tried and she went through the rest of her life carrying the family secret. She never dated, never got married, and never had children. She died internally that day.

When the event occurred Tamar ripped the garment that signified that she was a virgin, which tells us that as far as she was concerned she was now impure and unworthy to wear such a virtuous garment. Her own thinking concerning herself became warped from one single traumatic act that was not her fault. Can you relate to her? Her **Either/Or** thought was this: *"I can **Either** marry as a virgin (or as a respectable woman) who has never suffered a sexual violation, **Or** I can live in seclusion and bitterness, because I'm unworthy to have anything different."*

Many of you have experienced something similar, and you've been punishing yourself internally as a result. What happened to you doesn't define you. Jesus was crucified, but He is certainly not a victim and neither are you. Hold your head up high and receive the redemption Jesus died for you to have. If you were unworthy, certainly, no blood would've been shed on your behalf. God loves you in spite of your checkered past, and nothing can separate you from His love.

So, what do you think? With God on our side like this, how can we lose? If God didn't hesitate to put everything on the line for us, embracing our condition and exposing himself to the worst by sending his own Son, is there anything else he wouldn't gladly and freely do for us? And who would dare tangle with God by messing with one of God's chosen? Who would dare even to point a finger? The One who died for us—who was raised to life for us!—is in the presence of God at this very moment sticking up for us.

Do you think anyone is going to be able to drive a wedge between us and Christ's love for us? There is no way! Not trouble, not hard times, not hatred, not hunger, not homelessness, not bullying threats, not backstabbing, not even the worst sins listed in Scripture. . . None of this fazes us because Jesus loves us. I'm absolutely convinced that nothing—nothing living or dead, angelic or demonic, today or tomorrow, high or low, thinkable or unthinkable— absolutely nothing can get between us and God's love because of the way that Jesus our Master has embraced us. (Romans 8:31–39 MSG)

Unfortunately, Tamar was unaware of this kind of love, but you and I should be well-aware. God loves you! His love for you does not diminish because another person didn't value you enough to love you the same. Perhaps something terrible did happen to you. Maybe it's so traumatic that you could also say you suffered an internal death. But that does not have to be the end of your story. No matter what violations you have suffered, none of them are strong enough to destroy your life in Christ Jesus without your permission. Be relentless in your pursuit of greatness regardless of what you may have suffered. Jesus did it, and you are called to be like Him. His hopes concerning you are just and pure and full of a promising future (Jer. 29:11). He hasn't given up on you, and you shouldn't either. Lay aside those limiting **Either/Or** thoughts that have nothing to do with the plans God has for you and your future. Choose to embrace God's love for you.

Either/Or thoughts attempt to arise and take advantage of us is when we need to have strong faith.

❖ Sometimes **Either/Or** thoughts show up when we are presented with new opportunities.

Moses is a prime example of this. He was presented with the awesome opportunity to become the deliverer for God's chosen nation, Israel. For hundreds of years, they had been slaves in Egypt and God was now about to answer their prayers for freedom. However, just as Gideon thought he was at the bottom of the barrel because of his position in his family, Moses dealt with insecurities. His were not caused by his bloodline because he was raised in Egypt as a prince. Perhaps they were a result of guilt derived from his poor decision to kill an Egyptian, forcing him to flee town as a fugitive. Maybe it's because he was raised as an orphan because his parents had to give him up when he was young just to save his life. Maybe the seed of rejection was planted then and as an adult, his lack of judgment brought this chasm in his self-consciousness regarding his identity to the surface. Just like Tamar, his past produced a mindset that said he wasn't good enough to pursue big things.

But God! God had a different perspective of this man named Moses. God made His presentation and Moses' response was, "I am not qualified because I don't measure up to Pharaoh?" He began his reply in Exodus 3:11 with **"Who am I?"** If Moses knew who he was, he wouldn't have doubted God. Perhaps, it was the guilt from his past murder that hindered him. His **Either/Or** thought could have been: "Who am I Lord? I don't qualify to be a deliverer, because I'm a murderer. **Either** send someone else **Or** the people won't be delivered." The conversation progressed in

34

Exodus chapter 4. Let's examine Moses' excuses in vv. 1, 10, and 13 (MSG):

- v. 1   Moses objected, "They won't trust me. They won't listen to a word I say. They're going to say, 'GOD? Appear to him? Hardly!'"

- v. 10   Moses raised another objection to GOD: "Master, please, I don't talk well. I've never been good with words, neither before nor after you spoke to me. I stutter and stammer."

- v. 13   He said, "Oh, Master, please! Send somebody else!"

We must remember that when God calls us, He also qualifies us. Moses went on and on explaining his limitations to God as if He didn't already know what they were. Newsflash: God already knows your limitations and what you're bringing to the table—good and bad. He chose you anyway. This means, that whatever it is, it won't be a problem! Stop using it as an excuse. In response to Moses' complaint regarding his speech impediment, God told Moses to take Aaron with him to speak for him (vv. 14-17).

God's anger boiled against Moses, and He altered His plan to accommodate him. I don't want God to have to amend His plan to accommodate my stubbornness! I'm supposed to amend my plans to accommodate His plans. What's so dangerous about this is that our heavenly Father knows best and we don't. Moses thought he needed someone to go with him, but he didn't. Aaron was a major stumbling block to Moses many times throughout their journeys in the wilderness. He made a golden calf for the people to worship when Moses took too long to return from a prayer meeting, which led to the death of about 3,000 Israelites (Ex. 32:28). He came against Moses with Miriam because of the woman he chose to marry (Num. 12:1). Sure, he helped Moses, but he certainly hindered him as well. We must get rid of our limited thinking, because it will hinder our progress and potentially stunt our growth.

It's hard to serve the limitless God when we have limited thinking.

Not only can trauma or life-altering opportunities bring **Either/Or** thoughts to the surface, embarrassment or hurt feelings can as well.

❖ Sometimes **Either/Or** thoughts emerge through offense, misunderstanding or fear of judgment.

I believe that Peter is a prime example of this: It could be said that Peter was Jesus' right-hand man, who struggled like Moses. God described Moses as the friend he spoke with face-to-face (Ex. 33:11). And now Peter was a friend that Jesus always seemed to have around whenever anything exceptional happened. He was the first of the disciples to receive the revelation from Heaven that Jesus was indeed the Christ, the Son of the living God (Matt. 16:16). He was also present with Jesus at the mountain of transfiguration and was privileged to see Jesus in His glory speaking with Moses and Elijah (Mark. 9:2–5).

But something strange happened to Peter when Jesus was betrayed and was being questioned by the people. Shortly before that, Peter had boldly defended Jesus in the garden of Gethsemane by pulling out his sword and cutting off the ear of the servant of the high priest. Of course, Jesus rebuked him and put the man's ear back where it belonged totally healing him. Side note: I have always wondered why this miracle didn't cause those arresting Him to change their minds. But I'm glad they didn't because it would have interfered with God's plan to save us all (John 18:10–11, Luke 22:50–51, Isa. 53:10–11).

Perhaps, Peter was embarrassed by the way Jesus openly corrected him in front of everyone. While it wasn't the first time Jesus had corrected him, this was different. Peter was coming to Jesus' defense. He needed help, and Peter was the only one bold enough to fight off the guards. Jesus didn't appreciate it. I'm not sure if Peter really felt this way or not, but for some reason, all of his boldness left him when he was in the courtyard only moments after the garden incident. Maybe he was offended? Maybe he was scared?

Several people, one of them being a little girl, began saying he had been with Jesus and Peter vehemently denied it, so much so that he began to swear, possibly to prove that he was never with Jesus. He was almost successful but then it happened. . . . the cock crowed twice, just as Jesus had told him it would (Mark 14:72).

Has your denial of Christ ever crushed your spirit? Sure you were not in the courtyard of the high priest while Jesus was being betrayed but perhaps you've had other moments where your allegiance to Christ was tested Just as Peter's was. Maybe you didn't boldly proclaim your love for God in the breakroom at work when a co-worker was berating those "weak-brained Christians who can't think for themselves and need to go to church so their Pastor can give them direction." Or perhaps you downplayed your commitment to your volunteer service at your church when a friend of yours complained, "You live in church! That's all you do is go to church!" You knew that the correct answer is that you are actually a living, breathing organism that is the church. The Church is not something you do or a place you go but rather who you are due to your connection with Christ as a member of His body. But you chose to only smile and change the subject rather than get into a debate. I've been there, too. So what happens after this moment? Some of us, like Peter, retreat. We decide that we have let God down and that His Kingdom would be better off without us because we are more of a coward, backslider, or compromiser than a soldier.

Jesus, in His mercy and love for Peter didn't leave him in this state. After being raised from the dead, Jesus went to where Peter was: back on the Sea of Galilee fishing with the disciples. In life, when the unexpected happens, it's easy to revert back to what's comfortable or familiar. But if it means aborting our purpose for being, we have to resist the urge. Jesus had already told Peter to be a fisher of men, but he no doubt reasoned in himself that because he had deserted Jesus, he no longer "deserved" the high honor of being known as a disciple. His **Either/Or** thought sounded something like this: "I can **Either** follow hard after Christ, unwavering in my devotion, **Or** I can go back to what I was doing before because wavering in faith disqualifies me."

Many Christians may not admit it, but this is what causes some to backslide and leave the faith in the first place. They erroneously think that if they make a misstep in their walk with Christ that they are doing God a disservice and need to sever the relationship. This couldn't be further from the truth. And Jesus proved it when He restored Peter by giving him three opportunities to profess his love for Jesus just as he had three times denied ever knowing Him (John 21:17–19).

This time Peter got it right. He confessed his love for Christ and went on to demonstrate such power in his ministry that people received their healing from being in his shadow as he walked by (Acts 5:15). Like Peter, you, too, can renew your mind to the fact that despite your mistakes, personal offenses, and misunderstandings you may have had, even with God, He hasn't and will not throw you away.

Although **Either/Or** thoughts may try to rise up, you can resist them and go on to do many mighty things. Moses, Gideon, and Peter all eventually got it right. They resisted their insecurities, trusted in God, overcame their **Either/Or** thoughts, and moved forward to make history. Let's do the same.

It's hard to serve the limitless God when we have limited thinking.

Either/Or thoughts can also show up when well-meaning people in our lives believe they are trying to warn us or protect us.

❖ Sometimes friends or relatives who believe they are motivated by love will caution us from doing too much in the name of concern for our well-being, which may cause us to entertain **Either/Or** thoughts.

While the intentions of friends and family may be genuine, it doesn't necessarily mean that they're being led by God to say what they're saying. They could be motivated by fear that disguises itself as being concern. When they express their thought to us, it may be difficult for us to reject it because it is coming from a trustworthy and loving source. Jesus went through this from those closest to Him, and He knew better than to listen. Peter received the revelation directly from Heaven that Jesus was indeed the Christ, the Son of the living God and in the same moment was rebuked by Jesus when he presented his concern about Jesus' upcoming crucifixion (Matt 16:16-23).

The whole purpose for Jesus' birth was so He could die the death that He described to the disciples. Yet, Peter allowed his emotions to cloud his vision for God's purposes. Peter's selfish concern (not wanting to lose his friend whom he thought would establish an earthly kingdom) led him to fall into the hands of Satan who used him to try to discourage Jesus from fulfilling His destiny. If we're not careful, Satan will use us in a similar fashion to speak **Either/Or** thoughts of doubt into the lives of those we love as well.

This reminds me of the conversation I shared with you in Chapter 1. I do not believe that the woman who sincerely expressed her concern meant any harm. But her concern left me with many doubts and questions that discouraged me from pursing what was in my heart. I did indeed pursue it, but only after constantly challenging the **Either/Or** Thoughts that regularly bombarded my mind.

Additionally, to make matters worse, the **Either/Or** thought that "I was unable to be a successful wife, mother and minister all at the same time" was supported by the female examples that I knew personally or that I watched from afar through media while growing up. Most of the successful women I knew of were either single or childless or both. The women who had families were either working jobs they hated, instead of pursuing their dreams, or they were work-at-home moms. (I like to say, work-at-home moms, instead of stay-at-home moms because I now know that staying at home with children is WORK.)

At the time that I had the conversation with this well-meaning Christian, I only knew of one woman who was in ministry and doing well. She had her own products and business ventures that were successful and had a husband and children that seemed to be doing well, also. I truly believe God exposed me to this woman to show me that it was indeed possible to do **both** and that I didn't have to settle with **Either/Or**.

During the conversation I had with the **Either/Or** friend, I responded as kindly as I could to her concerns without saying too much. I was afraid that if I did, I might blast her for injecting more fear and doubt into my already troubled mind. My response was simple. I said that if God knew that giving me a husband and children would interfere with my ability to obey Him in the areas of ministry and business to which He called me, He would not have given me the family and the calling at the same time. He would have given these responsibilities to another woman that could handle them. The fact that God was the one leading me to pursue all of the above meant that it must be possible, and He'd assist me in fulfilling my call while still having a healthy, thriving marriage and a strong relationship with all of my God-fearing children. However, while I believed this with my heart, my head often wrestled with the what-ifs:

- **What if** I become this dynamic, world-shaking minister that drastically makes history in a positive way for the kingdom of God, changes lives, and blesses millions, but lose my marriage and family in the process?

- **What if** I pursue these business and career ventures that I believe God put in my heart, but stop being an active minister and in essence become a secular worker who has nothing to do with ministry or loses credibility in the religious world?

- **What if** I spend most of my time and energy cultivating my family and ensuring that my marriage is strong and my children develop into wonderful people who love God, but are unable to pursue ministry and other ventures with the same tenacity, and they fall by the wayside?

These what-ifs are not unique to me. I would dare say that most people, especially women, have them in some form as it relates to career and family. This brings me to some hard truths I had to acknowledge and process, and I hope my transparency helps you to process your truth as well.

Chapter 4 | The HARD Truth

"We must always remember that God 'is able to do exceedingly abundantly above all that we ask or think, according to the power that works in us' (Eph. 3:20). We cannot allow our finite human minds to limit Him in our thinking and believing."
John Bevere, Author of *Relentless*

The hard truth is that it took me about nine years to complete this book, because while I was trying to encourage you to get rid of your **Either/Or** mindsets, I was struggling with several of my own. While writing the previous chapters, I was 32 years old and pregnant with my third child. Well, at the time of this writing, I am 37 and have four children and yes, still in the process of writing this book. Why did it take so long . . . ? Remember how I encouraged you to stay connected to the Word, your Vine, Jesus Christ and press into the presence of Holy Spirit no matter how distracting life can be? Sadly, I didn't listen to my own advice.

It's one of the nuances of ministry. To be in my field can be deceiving. I work for a church, serve the church, talk about God, work for God, and lead people to God. And the tricky part is that a minister can be around God and help others get closer to Him while simultaneously get further from their own personal intimacy with Him. The work of the ministry replaces the relationship they once had with their Friend. I didn't think this would happen to me, but it did. The long road back has been full of potholes. And it's still a struggle not to regress.

In 2008, I was initially inspired to write this book. Clumsily, I began the quest and lacked the passion and zeal to maintain my stamina to set and even reach deadlines. My lack of productivity caused me to question if this was really the first book I was supposed to write. I mean, after all, I had other book ideas in my heart. If this book wasn't going anywhere, why couldn't I just begin one of those? But I couldn't, even though I wanted to. I had a strong knowing that this book had to be the first. I also knew that the **Either/Or** message was supposed to be my life's message—not only something I wrote about. And thus the struggle: I was trying to write about something to help others that I had never actually experienced myself.

It's like a personal trainer giving his clients tips on losing weight, while he himself is morbidly obese. People would benefit from the tips but the nagging truth of his own inability to work the principles he is teaching would certainly vex the trainer's soul . . . and so it was with me. How could I possibly, encourage anyone, male, female, youth, adult alike to go after all God had for them and refuse to settle for an **Either/Or** lifestyle when my entire life was submerged in **Either/Or** dogma?

I was living in contradiction to what I was writing, and my soul wouldn't permit me to betray true authenticity. Year after year I struggled to create sentences and consecutive thought that would capture the hearts and minds of the readers only to be thwarted along the way. I would take long sabbaticals between writing. And:

. . . days turned into weeks . . .

. . . weeks turned into months . . .

. . . months turned into years . . .

Sometimes complete years would pass without me typing a single word! How embarrassing to my internal ego! I frantically did things to attempt to slap myself out of lethargy and regain momentum on the quest to OBEY GOD! He told me He put me on the earth to write and by golly, write was what I was going to do!

- ❖ I had several chapters of the book edited by a professional editor so it would motivate me to press on and publish. But this accomplished . . . NOTHING!

- ❖ I told people in leadership around me that I was writing a book hoping that their accountability would give me the fire, drive, and stamina that I needed to push out this work. But this accomplished . . . NOTHING!

- ❖ I went to conferences and read literature on book writing and publishing. But this accomplished . . . NOTHING!

Year after year I sat in New Year's Eve church services embarrassed, defeated and ashamed, feeling like a monumental failure and like the servant who hid His Master's talent in Matthew 25:24-25. But you know what I never considered until several years after God's initial invitation to write? Perhaps God never intended for me to complete the work then.

47

God spoke to me about writing and spoke to me about **Either/Or** being my life's message not because He wanted me to create a literary masterpiece within six months to a year. But because He knew that this would spark a necessary journey on the inside of my heart that would lead me from such a barren place to a place of oasis on the inside.

> "If you can't keep your mind on your HOPES, you'll default to your fears, disappointments."
> Casey Treat, Pastor and Speaker at FX Conference 2013 (author emphasis)

Like the children of Israel, I wandered around internally for many years, questioning His promise, His direction, and complaining about the provision He did send. "What is this manna— this purpose God has given me? Write books? Can I do something else? **Either/Or**—what is that? Can I write about something else? Speak to women! What! Why!? I thought I was called to the entire body of Christ—men, too!?"

I spent years wearing a mask of security and confidence. The "ministry mask" I call it. Walking into my church, women's meetings and posting on my online book club's wall messages of hope, empowerment, and enlightenment while I myself was disillusioned and desperate to find some if any enjoyment in life. What was I doing? Seemingly, I was in my call while not really being in it. To outsiders I was obeying God by preaching, leading women, assisting my husband with his call to our church, and mothering our children in the ways of the Lord. And yes, I did do

48

all of those things. But in my heart, the main thing—to write and speak the truth in love with much conviction on the topics of which I wrote wasn't happening, and I knew it.

Furthermore, I resented having to complete additional tasks that seemingly pulled me away from completing my above listed mission. Why clean, cook, lead women's meetings, run departments, and build relationships, if I die and still never scratch the surface with what I was called to do? Everything seemed like a waste of time—like a major distraction from my life's mission. Ever been there before?

But now, I see much more clearly. These things were not distractions. All of the other things I am involved in, no matter how mundane or exciting they are, are all parts of my story. They are all valuable pieces working together to shape my perspectives and worldview that will in turn give me content and clarity through which I can now inform others.

For years passion for my assignment eluded me. I spent years angry with God for telling me what to do and then not providing the drive and passion for which to do it. I tried to conjure it up over and over again and failed. I could relate to Solomon's Ecclesiastes, what I think is the most depressing book of the Bible. Everything was vanity! My intimacy with God waned. Because how could I be intimately connected to God when I secretly resented Him?

Flippantly, I began calling myself Erica "Jonah" Moore. The prophet Jonah in scripture jumped into a boat headed in the opposite direction from the city to which he had been called.

Internally while it looked to others as if I were going the right way I was drifting further and further away from I AM (Jonah 1:1–3). I wish I could tell you that my journey back to intimacy with my King and authenticity with myself came back all at once and with ease, but it didn't. It took death to pride, admission of flawed thinking, a renewing of my mind, and an attack on my human will and flesh. It took reading books, such as *Living Life on Purpose* by Lysa TerKeurst, *The Emotionally Healthy Woman* by Geri Scazzaro, *12 Traits of the Greats* by Dr. Dave Martin and going through the exercises over and over.

Without compromise the solution was clear: I had to relinquish control of my image and open up and let others see the flaws I was hiding in order to build real relationships. It meant investing time to train up other leaders while I didn't feel like much of a leader myself. I encountered much loss on this journey: loss of sleep and loss of confidence. I lost time, wandering in self-pity.

Death took the lives of two women I loved so deeply; my grandmother and mother within the same year. Death took a few more unborn children through several miscarriages. Complaining took away joy. I could go on and on. So what was my moment of clarity? There was not one moment. There were many moments over the course of an 8-to-9-year span that brought me to this moment that I am now living and typing. Everyone's journey to fulfillment, peace, solace, and satisfaction is different. I've learned to stop looking for "the formula" and let what needs to happen simply happen.

God leads us to stop fighting, be still, and know that He is God (Psalm 46:10). This scripture is one the Holy Spirit brings to me often to help quiet the war in my head. Isn't it good to know that no matter how loud life gets, as His sheep, His promise to us is that we will still hear His voice? (John 10:27) You may be in a noisy field but your Shepherd knows how to get your attention. Won't you use the authority He's given you to silence the voices in your head that don't sound like His?

On a day that I was attempting to do this, I listened to a sermon by Willie George, the pastor of Church on the Move, called, "You Can Hear the Voice of God." In his message, he said, "Once God gives you a calling, He gives you the passion for it." I remember resenting this when I initially heard it because I was struggling to muster up passion to attend church services, and I was a pastor's wife for Pete's sake! Why didn't God give me passion when He spoke to me about becoming an author in 2008? I don't know fully, but guess what! Passion dropped into my lap at another dreaded New Year's Eve church service in 2016.

I sensed something different about to happen on the inside. I had been reading those books I mentioned, talking candidly to my husband about my internal issues, building teams in spite of my insecurities, and I could just sense something shifting. And then it happened. As the Word of the Lord went forth, I got excited about writing again. I knew that I knew that I

51

knew that I was going to complete this book! Not because my team held me accountable to some deadlines but because God was going to and had been taking me on a journey to fully realize the book's message. I came to realize while sitting in that blue padded seat that like King Solomon, I went through the toughest, bleakest times of my life just so I could come out reborn on the other side.

Let us hear the conclusion of the whole matter: Fear God, and keep his commandments: for this is the whole duty of man. (Ecclesiastes 12:13 KJV)

God dropped an excitement and zeal in my heart that I couldn't muster up on my own for eight years. I'm not saying not to try and not to pray and fast and do research when you're not "feeling it" because all of those things are good, and they can all lead to helping passion and fire arise. But what I've learned in my own life is that God is truly my Shepherd (Ps. 23). He leads me on paths I like and on paths that I don't. I won't always understand, agree with, or even enjoy the journey, but I should never leave my Shepherd. He knows what He's doing, and once I reach my destination, it always makes sense.

I pray that if you haven't learned this lesson yet, that you will soon. Pastor and author Dharius Daniels truly touched my life. He and his wife spoke to the women at my church about his book *Re-Present Jesus*. He said some things that struck me to the core and changed my life. It redefined my perspective on why it was taking me so long to complete this book. Dharius talked about how he would read the Word and would agree with what he read but realized that he wasn't living what he read. The joy he read about was not real in his own life. Dharius wanted to experience the fulfillment that the disciples had to the degree that they were willing to die tragic deaths because of what they had seen, experienced, and knew to be true concerning Jesus.

Dharius' quest of achieving sincerity brought him to the place where he could write and finish his book on demonstrating Christ's character authentically because he actually began to live a life that mirrored the image of what he was studying. I thought it was so profound that a man who taught the Bible every week for years found it to be a challenge to live authentically what he taught. And this had nothing to do with him being in sin.

He said that night at my women's meeting that he refused to write a book full of principles that he himself wasn't living. That struck a chord on the inside of me. That was my answer! I realized for the first time WHY it was taking me so long to complete this book, WHY I had major writers block, WHY I lacked the passion to complete it and didn't even want to write. I couldn't write about what I hadn't become.

My husband often says, "We can teach what we know, but we reproduce who we are." God didn't give me this assignment only to help others. He gave it to me because of what needed to happen in me. And it is the same with you. What God has given you is not just for others. It is first for you. Once I accepted this, the passion came and the work was completed. I always said, "The Workman is more important than the work" while simultaneously neglecting myself in the name of doing more work. How ironic!

So what has God spoken to you about? Are you still wrestling internally with the mechanics of it? Still questioning if you are the right person for the job? Are you allowing the Lord to be your Shepherd or do you shepherd yourself when you don't agree with a detour or a rout?

Self-Assessment

Please take a moment to answer the following questions. And don't be like me, the person who always skipped assessments in every book because I had things to do and didn't have the time. I would often skip the assessments at the end of chapters deceiving myself into thinking that I could fly through the chapters and would come back and do the assessments later. Of course, I never did and the nuggets of truth that impacted me initially were never applied. Do NOT be that person. I encourage you to read Psalm 23 and answer the following questions in a journal or notebook.

Questions

1) Have you been allowing God to be your Shepherd in all areas? If no, why do you think that is?

2) What areas do you need to allow Him to lead you more?

3) Why are you resisting His leading in those areas?

4) Do you feel scared or afraid? If so, put into words your feelings and what is causing them.

5) Find five scriptures that address this fear and read them aloud as often as you need to.

6) What do you need from God or from others to motivate you to follow Him, even blindly if necessary?

Chapter 5 | A New Dawn

> "Just like Peter, we must be willing to lose it all in order to make it." Sean R. Moore, Pastor of Faith Christian Center-Phoenix

The day Peter became a water-walking disciple is the day he decided that the risk didn't overshadow the benefits of the reward. The risk of embarrassment and even possible harm, didn't minimize the benefit of making human history and pursuing a journey walking towards Christ that he'd never experienced before. I wish the authors of the Gospel's would've included Peter's emotional, mental, and physical state after this event occurred in his life. Surely he had to be different. I mean, you don't just walk directly toward the King of kings, Lord of lords, The Way, The Truth and The Life, The Rose of Sharon, The Bright and Morning Star and come out completely the same on the other side.

I wonder if his internal wiring left him at an advantage or disadvantage after this encounter. Did he focus on the fact that even just for a moment, he defied gravity as a result of tapping into the supernatural law of faith by responding to one Word from God—come. Or did he focus on the rebuke that soon followed when Jesus escorted him back into the boat. "Oh you of little faith, why did you doubt?" (Matt. 14:31)

What about you? If/when you and God collaborate on an assignment, do you focus on the fact that the two of you did something great, even if only for a few seconds or do you focus

55

on your inability to withstand the pressures to quit or properly perform? Whichever one you focus on will determine if you go for it the next time. Ask yourself this:

- Does my thinking assist me in fulfilling my purpose?

- Or does it prevent me from even dreaming?

No Delete Button

I had to learn that part of the process of becoming a writer means that you have to learn how to just write without editing and deleting the not-so-good moments on the page. If a writer edits while he or she writes, they may become discouraged along the way and never complete the project. Jesus already edited your story when He died on the cross for you. God doesn't need you to assist Him with the masterpiece of the storyline of your life. All of the scenes that you would like to delete will flow nicely into the whole and He is not surprised that they occurred. While they may not have been perfect or even pleasant, they all together have brought you to this point. And if you trust the Master, He's an expert at taking a mess and creating something beautiful to be admired and even celebrated.

Will you let Him do that with your life? Will you make the commitment to align your thoughts, your speech, and finally your actions with His Word and His personal plans for your life? I hope you said yes! The fact that you're reading this book shows me that you know there is more to life than simply existing, having good times with your friends and family, paying bills and taking care of obligations and responsibilities. No. You know that God never wastes anything or anyone. The fact that you are on this planet points to the fact that greatness is on the inside of you. I'm excited that you are willing to embark on a journey of mind renewal. This journey as spoken of in Romans 12 is not just a daily, weekly or monthly one. It will last your entire life.

And do not be conformed to this world, but be transformed by the renewing of your mind, that you may prove what is that good and acceptable and perfect will of God.
(Romans 12:2)

God needs to rewire us like a determined hair stylist tediously untangling knots in a child's hair. While the process may seem unpleasant and we might just be tempted to speed things along by grabbing the scissors and cutting away, it might not be the best option. Do you trust that God's plans for you are better than your own? The Lord thinks so, "For I know the thoughts that I think towards you, says the Lord, thoughts of peace and not of evil, to give you a future and a hope." (Jeremiah 29:11 NKJV) This has always been one of my favorite scriptures and I've quoted it since I was a child. Yet as an adult, my thoughts seemed to contradict what I knew to be true in my heart. Here are some of the **Either/Or** thoughts that I had concerning ministry that hindered me from pursing my individual purpose and led to the delay of completing this book:

- I can **Either** hide behind a mask of "everything is OK with me and my life," **Or** the church is going to fall apart.

- I can **Either** put on my confident, "God is in control, nothing is bothering me" ministry mask in order to properly serve the people, **Or** I can be fully transparent and risk losing their respect and become an ineffective leader.

- I can **Either** violate my need for solitude to meet everyone's social need **Or** stay selfishly to myself while my congregation is denied the right to connect with me.

I even had **Either/Or** thoughts in relation to parenting that caused me to squander my time rather than spend it wisely. These too resulted in guilt, grief, and wasted time that could've been avoided. They were:

- I can **Either** put my foot down and force the kids to do chores and deal with their resentment, **Or** I can grumble under my breath while doing all of the chores myself, aiding my kids in becoming lazy.

- I can **Either** begin to trust others to watch my children and put them in harm's way, **Or** I can always keep them with me, and miss tons of social events and date nights with my husband.

It took me years to accurately identify these thoughts and finally challenge and dismantle them. And trust me, I have not arrived. I will always have to intentionally renew my mind and hold tightly to what I have learned.

Therefore we ought to give the more earnest heed to the things which we have heard, lest at any time we should let them slip.

(Hebrews 2:1 KJV)

In the following chapters, I will share the truths I choose to embrace to make permanent mind renewal possible. I expect them to be as beneficial to you in your own life. But before we move on, I want you to take a moment and list your biggest **Either/Or** thoughts in a journal or notebook:

I can **EITHER** _____ **OR** _____ .

I can **EITHER** _____ **OR** _____ .

I can **EITHER** _____ **OR** _____ .

I can **EITHER** _____ **OR** _____ .

I can **EITHER** _____ **OR** _____ .

Chapter 6 | How To Get Rid Of **Either/Or** Thoughts?

For the weapons of our warfare are not carnal but mighty in God for pulling down strongholds, casting down arguments and every high thing that exalts itself against the knowledge of God, bringing every thought into captivity to the obedience of Christ.
(2 Corinthians 10:4–5)

"Stronghold" as defined by *Merriam-Webster Dictionary* is a place where a particular cause or belief is strongly defended or upheld. The Strong's Concordance defines it as an argument or castle that we hold safely. It is essentially a fortified philosophy that we guard in our minds. This happens when we allow thoughts to take up residence for long periods of time without getting the bulldozer of the Word to knock them down. Believers must become skilled at using the Word of God to knock down the walls of negative, wrong, self-defeating thinking designed to hinder us from achieving, receiving, living, and giving God's best.

Removing EITHER/OR Strongholds

1. Cast Down the Wrong Thoughts or Imaginations

Take a moment to look at 2 Corinthians 10:4-5 again.

This verse makes it clear that we are involved in a warfare that it is not physical. Because it is not a physical battle, our weapons that we use to win cannot be physical either. Our weapons come from God and they allow us to pull down or dismantle strongholds—things that have a gritty grip on our minds. They are described as imaginations or thoughts that attempt to hold higher regard or authority in our lives than our knowledge of God does. We are instructed to aggressively attack these thoughts—the ones that don't agree with God's instructions—and command them to be in subjection to Christ.

It is clear that the responsibility of taking ownership of our thoughts is ours and not God's. He has given us weapons. According to Ephesians 6:10–17, we have been given the:

- **Word of God:** The <u>sword</u> we use to cut our enemy.

- **Faith:** Our <u>shield</u> that protects us from the arrows of life.

- **Truth**: Our <u>belt</u> that ensures the rest of our armor stays in place.

- **Gospel of Peace:** The <u>shoes</u> for our feet as we progress in our callings.

- **Righteousness:** Our <u>breastplate</u> protecting our hearts.

- **Salvation:** Our <u>helmet,</u> covering our most valuable asset, our reasoning faculty.

No good soldier goes into battle half-dressed and neither should we. It is our decision to make. We can either leave our homes fully clothed, scantily clad or totally naked. But if we expect to win the battlefield of the mind, we need to be properly dressed at all times.

The Word of God is our sword and it helps us to cut through the jungle of thoughts that crowd out the light of the Gospel as we live in a degenerated world. Jesus is described in scripture as the Word of God and the Light of the World at the same time. If we want light, revelation, insight, clarity and hope in our lives, we must first get some light in our thoughts because as a man thinks in his heart, so is he (Prov. 23:7). Remember when God restored the earth to its proper state in Genesis? He first said, "Light be!" and what He spoke happened. Light or revelation could not exist until He commanded it to be so with His mouth, and we are to be imitators of him as dear children (Eph. 5:1).

If He <u>spoke,</u> <u>saw</u> and then said it was <u>good,</u> then we too must <u>speak and</u> we'll <u>see</u> what we say and it will be <u>good</u> for us as well.

*Therefore <u>take no thought,</u> **saying**, What shall we eat? or, What shall we drink? or, Wherewithal shall we be clothed? (Matthew 6:31 KJV, author emphasis)*

We embrace thoughts by speaking them. We cast them down by speaking against them. The power you need is in your mouth.

Words kill, words give life; they're either poison or fruit— you choose. (Proverbs 18:21 MSG)

Let me share a story with you to illustrate how easy it can be to take authority over the wrong thoughts with our own words. I have taught my kids how to get rid of the pervasive thoughts preventing them from going back to sleep after having a bad dream. They are to wake up and speak the opposite of whatever they saw in the dream. For example, Heaven had a dream once that she and her siblings got lost in a crowded mall and that I either couldn't find them or I left them. So I told her to speak the opposite and she said, "I thank you Jesus that we'll never get lost in a mall and that mommy and daddy will never leave us." We need to do the same thing. If the pervasive thought in your mind is, "I don't have enough money coming in to make the black this year where my business is concerned," then you say, "I thank you God that you supply all of my need according to your riches in glory by Christ Jesus, and I will finish this year in the black." (Phil. 4:19).

You may be asking, "But isn't it good enough to just think that in your head? Why is there a need to say it aloud?" Well, for one thing, it's important that you hear yourself saying it (especially if you're quoting the Word) because faith comes by hearing and hearing by the Word of God (Rom. 10:17). And secondly, Satan, is not a mind reader. God is all-knowing or omniscient; the devil is not. So he can't hear you attacking his negative thoughts if you don't do so aloud. If you say nothing, he'll get encouraged, assuming his assault is working and the thoughts will continue to come at an even faster, stronger, regular pace. Remember, if we resist the devil, he will flee, but not if we ignore or tolerate him (James 4:7). Let him know that you are alert and vigilant; that you recognize what he's attempting to do and pierce him through with the sword of the Spirit being released from your mouth, which is the Word of God.

For the word of God is quick, and powerful, and sharper than any two-edged sword, piercing even to the dividing asunder of soul and spirit, and of the joints and marrow, and is a discerner of the thoughts and intents of the heart. (Hebrews 4:12 KJV)

2. No More Negative Self-Talk

In order to get rid of **Either/Or** Thoughts, we must eliminate negative self-talk. It has been said that we believe our own voice more than we believe anyone else's, even God's. This makes reading the Word aloud and confessing specific promises from the Word aloud critically important. I encourage you to record yourself saying what God has promised you either directly through prophecy, dreams, visions or in your personal study time. Also record yourself reading the scriptures that speak to your situation specifically. Play it several times daily until you begin to believe what you hear about yourself. If you don't go that route, you can read your positive affirmations to yourself aloud and/or say them while looking at yourself in the mirror. Even unbelievers do this and see miraculous results because death and life are in the power of the tongue (Prov. 18:21).

Our words are life-giving and powerful. They can construct our worlds or dismantle them. I had a college professor who bragged every class period of how he had "cured himself of cancer". Yes, cancer. He attributed his recovery, not to an awesome God who heals, saves, and delivers, and not even to medical breakthroughs, but to his positive daily confessions. He said that he would say every day, multiple times a day, "I don't have cancer," along with other positive affirmations. He did this for months at strategic times of the day, every day and the cancer vanished. Now, if a person who doesn't acknowledge that God is the healer, that Jesus bore our sicknesses and diseases, and doesn't confess Him as his Savior can walk in that level of physical manifestation to the degree that a disease he once had vanishes, then certainly the children of the Light can and should do the same! Something I constantly tell my children when I hear them whining and complaining or worrying about something is:

"Say What You Want, Not What You Don't Want!"

But no one can tame the human tongue; it is a restless evil [undisciplined, unstable], full of deadly poison. With it we bless our Lord and Father, and with it we curse men, who have been made in the likeness of God. Out of the same mouth come both blessing and cursing. These things, my brothers, should not be this way [for we have a moral obligation to speak in a manner that reflects our fear of God and profound respect for His precepts]. (James 3:8–10 AMP)

Self-Inventory

Write your responses to the following question in a journal or notebook.

Q) How often do you think or say things like this about yourself? (Use the scale 1 through 5; 1=never, 5=constantly, 3=every now and then.

- I'm so stupid.
- It's too late for me; my time has passed.
- No one will want me now.
- I'm going to live from paycheck to paycheck for the rest of my life.
- I'm so ugly, fat, unattractive (you fill in the blank).
- I'll never get a job.
- No one loves me.
- No one understands me.
- I made my bed now I have to lie in it.
- I must be getting punished for something I did in my past.
- I deserve it (all the bad things that have or are happening).

You were made in the image and likeness of God and don't have the right to curse verbally or even internally what He has already blessed! Stop respecting strangers and treating others better than you treat yourself. My friend Audrey Meisner taught me in her book *Like Yourself, Love Your Life* to treat myself like I would my best friend. Most of us wouldn't dream of addressing people the way we address ourselves even in our own thoughts. You are fearfully and wonderfully made, which is precious and

67

beautiful in the sight of God and washed spotless in the blood of the lamb. Speak blessings only and not curses over yourself!

If you're anything like me, you'll catch yourself saying things aloud about yourself that don't align with scripture. For instance, if I accidentally drop a few items in a row in a clumsy fit and wind up staining the carpet, I may mumble "Ugh! So stupid!" but immediately, I'll follow it up with, "No, I'm not stupid, I have the mind of Christ. I just made a mistake that's all."

"But Erica, does it really take all of that? Come on. The carpet?" YES! If you expect to live the life God has put you on this earth to live—free from limited thinking and expression in your everyday experiences—it will take all of that and MORE!

3. Surround Yourself With the Right People

I cannot emphasize enough how important it is to keep the right company of people around you. In Acts 3, Peter and John ministered healing to a lame man who begged at the Gate Beautiful for money. He had been lame since his birth, and this miracle caused no small stir. Peter and John gave all the credit to Jesus, saying that He was the Son of God and risen from the dead, infuriating the religious leaders.

So on the next day, the leaders convened and decided to forbid Peter and John from ever preaching or teaching about Jesus ever again and this is where the story gets really good. Peter and John didn't cower away and say, "OK, maybe this is God's will? We thought He called us to preach the good news, that Jesus is the Messiah, crucified and risen from the dead with all power in His hands, but we must be mistaken. If it was God's will for us to preach, He would protect us but here we are in danger. Let's just go back and tell everyone what has happened and hang it up and go back to leading normal lives." Thank goodness this wasn't their response and it should not be ours when things get tough. Hold fast to the gift of God within you and demonstrate that gift with boldness. We'll pick up with the story in v. 23 after the rulers had again forbidden them from preaching to Gospel:

After Peter and John were released, they returned to their own [people] and reported everything that the chief priests and elders had said to them. And when they heard it, they raised their voices together to God. (Acts 4:23–24a AMP)

Notice what happened! After they had been threatened, they RETURNED TO THEIR OWN PEOPLE. And notice what their group did in v. 24: THEY LIFTED THEIR VOICES TOGETHER WITH ONE UNITED MIND TO GOD. You and I need to travel through life with a group of people who are united in the decision to follow HARD, not casually, after the things of God regardless of the consequences. Just think if Peter and John had surrounded themselves with cowardly or compromising Christians who valued their own comfort and safety over getting the Gospel message out. They may have been wrongly influenced to turn in their minister's cards. But instead, they were emboldened in their faith and strengthened because they surrounded themselves with the right people. The spreading of the Gospel could have ended right then and if so, you and I may not have ever heard it. But instead, it spread like wildfire because the early church was united in the faith and the Apostles kept the right company. Just look at the result of their prayer:

While they were praying, the place where they were
meeting trembled and shook. They were all filled with the
Holy Spirit and continued to speak God's Word with
fearless confidence. The whole congregation of believers
was united as one-one heart, one mind! They didn't even
claim ownership of their own possessions. Not one said,
'That's mine; you can't have it.' They shared everything.
The apostles gave powerful witness to the resurrection of
the Master Jesus, and grace was on all of them.
(Acts 4:31–33 MSG)

God met the spiritual, physical and financial needs of the early church simply because they kept the right people around them. Like Peter and John, you have greatness on the inside of you that can either be nurtured or stifled by those you chose to be around. Guard your heart with all diligence and choose your friends wisely. Make sure that the ones you're surrounded by don't add negative **Either/Or** thoughts into your mind. If they do, you should end the relationship altogether or severely limit the amount of time you spend with them so that their negative influence doesn't hinder God from being able to express the totality of His nature in and through you. Now if this person is your spouse or a close relative, like a parent, this is easier said than done. But it is possible.

I'm not telling you to divorce your spouse or to never visit your parent, but I am telling you to prepare your heart in advance for the interactions you'll have with this person. Even if after speaking to them about certain things, you have to respectfully leave the room and look in the mirror and recite your positive affirmations to cancel out the negative words that were said, do what you gotta do! You are worth it and your destiny is too important to be tampered with. You owe it to God and yourself to live out your God-given potential. Greatness is in you. Be determined to let it out!

You can be freed from Either/Or Thinking! Being around the right people will certainly help. I am sure you may be able to think of more ways to get freed from **Either/Or** Thinking but I'm only going to share one more.

4. Develop Discriminating Senses

In order to develop discriminating senses, you have to become selective concerning what you'll allow yourself to watch, listen to, and participate in. I know you're grown and you can watch sexually charged or fear-driven movies, listen to sad songs, watch plays shrouded with anger and limitation, read novels stooped in betrayal and envy, have conversations about how the government isn't doing enough to stimulate the economy, but this may not be advantageous for your soul, particularly for your mind. If you are going to have success in detoxing your thinking from the wrong **Either/Or** Thoughts, you certainly don't need to engage in activities that put them there.

Keep thy heart with all diligence; for out of it are the issues of life. Put away from thee a froward mouth, and perverse lips put far from thee. Let thine eyes look right on, and let thine eyelids look straight before thee. Ponder the path of thy feet, and let all thy ways be established. Turn not to the right hand nor to the left: remove thy foot from evil.
(Proverbs 4:23–27 KJV)

Now let's look at each verse again with the definitions inserted from the Strong's Concordance along with translation:

71

- v. 23: Keep (guard, protect and maintain) your heart (feelings, will, intellect, understanding) with all diligence (like a guard at the post of a prison); because out of it comes the boundaries, source and exits of life.

This verse says that the condition of our heart will determine what we experience in life because our boundaries or limitations or sources of exits (our ability to leave a bad situation and or enter a new, positive one) is determined by our hearts. Therefore, it becomes necessary that we protect our heart along with its feelings, its desires, and its understandings like a person guarding the post of a prison.

Imagine a prison guard casually drifting asleep with the safety off of his firearm and the keys to the prison dangling aimlessly within the reach of the most notorious prisoner. Soon, that guard will most likely lose his life as those bound quickly escape and wreak havoc over the city. And so it will be with us if we fail to maintain watch over our own hearts. Those criminal things that we thought we had bound in chains to never hurt us again (like the pain of past abuse or the memory of betrayal) will once again, re-emerge with the intent to do us harm. This is why it becomes so important that we honor v. 24 and do what it says whether it is convenient, easy, or popular to do or not.

- v. 24: Put away (depart from and remove from you) a forward and perverse (or perverted) type of speech – see to it that you (withdraw from that kind of speaking and widen the distance between you and that kind of language).

Now, why is this so important? How can the words we choose to release from our mouths be so detrimental or beneficial to our hearts? Well, in Prov. 23:7, it says that as a man thinks in his heart, so is he. And both Matthew 12:34 and Luke 6:45 say that out of the abundance of the heart the mouth speaks. You can tell what's in a person's heart by what they allow to be spoken with their mouths.

Perception is everything. If you see yourself like a tiny grasshopper going up against some big giants in an unknown land, then you'll say things like, "I can't do it!" A person like this will run from their own triumphant battle for several years even though they've already been granted the victory in Christ Jesus. This is what the children of Israel did in the wilderness. But if this same person perceives that they are well-able or qualified to do what God has instructed them to do because He has equipped them by His grace, then just like Joshua and Caleb, they'll boldly shout, "We are well able, let us go up at once!" even in the face of doubt, fear and unbelief (Num. 13:30). Proverbs 4:25 says "Let your eyes, (knowledge, resemblance and regard) look right on (or directly in front of you)." Paul put it this way:

Brethren, I count not myself to have apprehended: but this one thing I do, forgetting those things which are behind, and reaching forth unto those things which are before, I press toward the mark for the prize of the high calling of God in Christ Jesus.
(Philippians 3:13–14)

In order to move forward in life, we must be looking forward. We cannot fix our gaze on the things we regret concerning our past if we expect to gain momentum in our pursuit of the destiny before us. It's similar to running in a race but turning your head to look at your competitors behind you instead of focusing on the finish line. My daughter Heaven ran track for a season and was pretty good at it, too. But every now and then, she did something that annoyed her coaches and me to no end, although we still got a chuckle out of it. When she got out in front of everyone else, she would start to look behind her to see where her competitors were. Frantically, we would all scream, "look straight ahead, keep going" as we saw her pace slightly slowing down with every sideways glance. We were finally able to convince her that running her race had more to do with her beating her fastest time than it did beating the girls running next to her. And this is a lesson for us as well.

Stop comparing your pace with your neighbors. You are in different lanes, pursuing different goals. Look straight ahead and press forward. Every sideways glance, fleeting thought that you ignore and allow to stay, could cost valuable seconds, which, in turn, could dramatically alter the results of your race. Cast them down, run toward your goal and enjoy your race.

"Ponder (revolve or relay or consider) the path of thy feet (or the direction or road you're traveling on), and let all thy ways (actions, conversations and the manner in which you travel through life) be established (proper, prosperous and stable)."

(Proverbs 4:26 KJV)

We could say it this way, "Determine wisely which direction your life is headed in. In order to steer correctly, all of your actions, conversations and mannerisms need to be appropriate to that of a man or woman of God."

- v. 27 "(Once you've determined the appropriate way to travel through life according to what is becoming of a Christ Follower), do not be moved to the left or the right and (withdraw) your direction in life from that which is evil, (harmful and wrong)."

This is why it's so important that we are very selective with what we allow our senses to feast on. The wrong diet can leave us in a lethargic state, unaware that the wrong thoughts are getting the best of us and having an effect on how we perceive the world.

"God expects believers to see the world through the lens of the Word, and not to see the Word through the lens of the world."
Sean R. Moore, Senior Pastor of Faith Christian Center-Phoenix

In order to have eyes and ears that are choosy in what they will pay attention to and allow to influence them, we have to maintain strict boundaries in place that we do not cross. What do I mean? Well, you and I know what our strengths and weaknesses are. Foreign substances have never been tempting to me. I have never felt an urge to get drunk, drink casually or experiment with illegal substances. So for me, watching a movie about narcotics and addiction may not be a big deal. But if you are a recovering addict, you might not want to watch that movie. It may rekindle the fire on the inside of you that you already extinguished. But for me, the opposite sex is attractive. When I was single, I chose to

75

limit the amount of sex, I mean, love songs I listened to and chick flicks involving passionate lust, I mean, love scenes I watched. Don't feed your flesh or (human nature without God) with frivolous entertainment or it may morph into an unruly beast on you!

For he who sows to his own flesh (lower nature, sensuality) will from the flesh reap decay and ruin and destruction, but he who sows to the Spirit will from the Spirit reap eternal life. (Galatians 6:8 AMP)

Train your eyes and ears to discriminate between what is good and evil and only entertain that which is good.

Is it not the task of the ear to discriminate between [wise and unwise] words, just as the mouth distinguishes [between desirable and undesirable] food? (Job 12:11 AMP)

Everything, even entertainment, has a voice and don't naively think that the enemy is not attempting to "program" you with his messages as you are casually enjoying "art".

There are, it may be, so many kinds of voices in the world, and none of them is without signification. (1 Corinthians 14:10 KJV)

Just because something is technically legal doesn't mean that it's spiritually appropriate. If I went around doing whatever I thought I could get by with, I'd be a slave to my whims. (1 Corinthians 6:12 MSG)

Bottom-line believer: Just because you can watch it, can listen to it, and can participate in it, doesn't mean you should. We should let God's Word have the loudest voice in our lives and systematically mute the voices that contradict God's will for our lives.

Chapter 7 | Whose Mind Should We Have?

"We've been preaching character, preaching character, preaching character. It's not about preaching right living; it's about preaching right believing. When you believe right, you will live right, you'll receive right, everything will be alright."
Joseph Prince, Senior Pastor of New Creation Church

Let this mind be in you which was also in Christ Jesus.
(Philippians 2:5)

According to scripture, we should allow or let the mind and thinking of Jesus Christ operate in our minds. This means that we must give Jesus' thoughts detailed in the scriptures the permission to permeate our own to the degree that our minds resemble His. It is possible to be a born-again, believing Christian who loves God with all of our heart but still have a mind that doesn't line up with scripture and doesn't resemble Christ's mind. If this is the case, confusion will come. How do we get the mind of Christ? We must go to Him.

Anyone you hang around will rub off on you. So if you hang around negative people, negativity will try to attach itself to you. If you hang around angry people, anger will try to attach itself to you. If you hang around silly people who play pranks on others and are always making people laugh, don't be surprised if your own sense of humor doesn't get boosted. We've all seen the good kid who hung around the wrong crowd and was wrongfully influenced. Hopefully, you've seen the reverse situation where a troubled kid got around the right influences and started to progress in life and make better decisions. There is no better influence than God and He invites us to hang out with Him.

> *Then Jesus said, 'Come to me, all of you who are weary and carry heavy burdens, and I will give you rest. Take my yoke upon you. Let me teach you, because I am humble and gentle at heart, and you will find rest for your souls. For my yoke is easy to bear, and the burden I give you is light. (Matthew 11:28–30 NLT)*

Well, it sounds easy enough, right? When your life becomes a heavy burden around your neck, go to Jesus, the one who gives rest. He'll exchange your yoke for His as you get more revelation of who He is and how much He loves you and has already provided. As a result, your mind, will, and emotions will get some rest. Because although Jesus does expect you to go through life managing purpose and responsibilities, the ones He assigns are easy and not bothersome.

It sounds like God has given us a square deal on life. It sounds like gold! So, why don't we "come to Him" initially when things get a little hairy in our lives even internally? I know what you're thinking, "I do go to God. I pray every day!" I don't doubt that if you call yourself a Christian that you speak to God daily and this is good. However, I have come to observe that many believers, myself included, tend to go to Christ for the solution to life's problems typically after they've consulted others or even their own opinions first and find that those options are lacking. We as believers have to learn to consult God first through reading

His Word, researching His heart and mind, "learning of Him" as He said in the above passage. This is the only practice that GUARANTEES us the mental and emotional "break" or "rest" we need. Everything else:

- Talking to a friend

- Reading a book

- Going to a seminar

- Watching a movie

- Buying something we want

- Engaging in a hobby

. . . might prove to be entertaining and even get our mind off of our problems, fears, and insecurities for a little while. But none of these options or even others like it, however, promise REST or PEACE. And isn't this really what we are all after?

You will keep him in perfect <u>peace</u>, whose <u>mind</u> is stayed on You: because he trusts in You.
(Isaiah 26:3 emphasis mine)

Wow! Perfect peace, huh!? What would that look like in your life? Take a moment to visualize this, Close your eyes and get a mental picture. What does perfect peace where you are concerned look like? Is it an absence of problems? I assure you that although that is a typical response, it is an unrealistic one since we live in a fallen world and have an enemy roaming around as a roaring lion seeking whom he may devour (1 Pet. 5:8).

What leads to complete peace of heart and mind? Keeping our thoughts centered on Jesus. Why? Because when we do this, it is an indication of our trust, our faith and our firm persuasion that what Jesus promised us, He has already provided and performed. Who wouldn't have peace after this!? I mean Jesus basically gave us a money back guarantee!

These things I have spoken to you, that in Me you may have peace. *In the world you will have tribulation; but be of good cheer; I have overcome the world.*
(John 16:33 emphasis mine)

The "these things" Jesus spoke about in this passage are the things that threaten our sanity and mind: He was telling the disciples that their faith or assurance in what they once believed to be true, (that He was the answer to all the world's problems) was going to be shattered and that they would be scattered. And they were when he was arrested and crucified. They never expected this to happen. They had left their families, businesses and lives as they knew it to follow the hottest new preacher in town and here he was . . . dead! It seemed like a catastrophically bad decision on their part to follow Jesus.

And sometimes, life leaves us feeling this way. Some unexpected tragedy occurs or some sought after desire never comes and it can leave us feeling hopeless, abandoned, and wanting. But in this same acknowledgement of trial, Jesus says that in the midst of this, we can still have peace and joy because He has already overcome the world.

Life is all about perspective. We can focus on the trial or we can focus on the lawyer we have working with us in God almighty to see us through. When we judge His track record in the scripture and in our own lives, we can plainly see that although we might not always understand or agree with His decisions, He is always faithful to His promise and His plans for us are for peace.

For I know the thoughts that I think toward you, says the LORD, thoughts of peace and not of evil, to give you a future and a hope. (Jeremiah 29:11)

Peace in Jeremiah 29, in John 16, and in Isaiah 26 comes from the Hebrew word Shalom and the Greek word Eirene (Power Bible CD 5.9)

- Shalom – Well, happy, friendly, great health, prosperity, safety and rest.

- Eirene – Quietness, rest, to set at one again.

Life can throw us curve balls that threaten to disturb our happiness, health, rest, safety and quietness of mind, but Jesus has promised us that we don't have to be disturbed if we make our thoughts focus on Him. Again it is our responsibility. Jesus is known as the Prince of peace. If He is your Lord, then peace—His peace—belongs to you.

Peace I leave with you; My [own] peace I now give and bequeath to you. Not as the world gives do I give to you. Do not let your hearts be troubled, neither let them be afraid. [Stop allowing yourselves to be agitated and disturbed; and do not permit yourselves to be fearful and

Notice that Jesus didn't give us hand-me-down peace; He gave us HIS peace. Jesus was able to calm a literal raging storm by simply saying, 'Peace be still" (Mark 4:39). He was able to simply walk through crowds that were trying to throw him off cliffs without being afraid or hurt (Luke 4:29). He was able to endure intense levels of misunderstandings and scrutiny without allowing it to damage his self-image or interfere with him accomplishing his goals.

And this is the same wonderful, mighty, magnificent savior that has given you and I—HIS PEACE! We have the peace of God and the mind of Christ. So if we go through life feeling like we're losing our minds or have no peace, we either don't know what Jesus has already done for us or we have forgotten and need to be reminded. Let this book be your reminder today! Jesus left you His peace: happiness, great health, prosperity, safety, rest and I love this truth: He has set you at one again. If your thoughts, emotions, decisions, and well-being has been divided and all over the place, then run back to Jesus because He has already made you one—sound and whole again.

Because of this understanding, we can obey the third sentence listed in John 14:27. We give ourselves no permission to have troubled and worried hearts, and we don't allow ourselves to stay afraid. I say "stay afraid" because fear may come. But because fear does come, doesn't mean we have to allow it to stay. Take charge over those thoughts of fear by replacing them with

God's thoughts toward you. Say the scriptures aloud concerning you and tell the fear who is boss. You have the mind of Christ so make sure you don't let anything or anyone, including yourself pressure you to lose your Christ-given mind!

Now, let's examine the kind of mind Jesus had because this is the kind of mind we are instructed to have, keep, and maintain.

Let this mind be in you which was also in Christ Jesus, who, being in the form of God, did not consider it robbery to be equal with God, but made Himself of no reputation, taking the form of a bondservant, and coming in the likeness of men. And being found in appearance as a man, He humbled Himself and became obedient to the point of death, even the death of the cross. Therefore God also has highly exalted Him and given Him the name which is above every name, that at the name of Jesus every knee should bow, of those in heaven, and of those on earth, and of those under the earth, and that every tongue should confess that Jesus Christ is Lord, to the glory of God the Father.
(Philippians 2:5–11)

So let's break this down. This is how God wants us to think. We understand that we are made in God's form and so we don't have a problem with believing that we are heirs of God and therefore entitled to His best. (Jesus didn't think it was wrong to be considered equal with God.) And we are joint heirs with Christ so we shouldn't have a problem receiving His best for our lives. This puts an end to accepting mediocre or worse things, reasoning that we don't "deserve" God's best anyway. This is not true humility. Jesus wasn't in pride or in sin for believing He was equal to God and thus acting that way. Similarly, we are not in pride or in sin for believing that we are covenant partners with God. It is time for us to believe and live out this truth.

Jesus was secure in His identity to the degree that He took on the form of a servant and even surrendered to death in order to fulfill his purpose for being on earth but never lost sight of who He was. Similarly, we, because we have His mind, can humble ourselves to do jobs or complete tasks or fulfill rolls that are seemingly "beneath us" and do it with a great attitude, never losing sight of our own value and purpose. Because Jesus did this, He was rewarded immensely. And if we operate with His mind and not the mind of society, our family traditions, or our own opinions, we will be immensely rewarded, also.

For who has known the mind of the Lord that he may instruct him? But we have the mind of Christ.
(1 Corinthians 2:16)

Woah! Did you see that? Paul told the Corinthian church that they "have" present tense, the mind of Christ. Not that they would be given it 10 years later after completing some intense Bible College or discipleship program. He said they had it already. This is amazing but what is disturbing is that one verse over, in chapter three of first Corinthians Paul says that he was unable to speak to them like they were mature believers but like they were baby Christians. And he goes on through the chapter to describe their selfish behavior and strife with other believers.

So does this mean that we can walk around housing the mind of Christ but still operate like babies that have to be treated like children, not mature enough to steward adult things? Yes, it

84

does. Having the mind of Christ and believing we have the mind of Christ, which in turn affects our thoughts and behavior, are two different things. We have to daily choose to operate in the peace and in the mind of Jesus no matter what is going on within us or around us. If it were impossible to do, Jesus would have never instructed us to do it. You can get rid of your **Either/Or** mindsets and all forms of limiting thinking. And you can keep those thoughts gone for good. The question is, will you do it?

Chapter 8 | What Thoughts Should We Think?

"Sometimes people try to think new things without replacing them with new thoughts."
Sean R. Moore, Senior Pastor of Faith Christian Center-Phoenix

To this point in the **Either/Or** mind renewal, we have:

- Defined **Either/Or** thinking.

- Explained how **Either/Or** thoughts develop.

- Strategized methods to uproot those thoughts and prevent new ones from being formed.

- Discussed the process of mind renewal to have Christ's mind.

But what should we be thinking about? I'm so glad you asked. Jesus said:

Finally, brethren, whatever things are true, whatever things are noble, whatever things are just, whatever things are pure, whatever things are lovely, whatever things are of good report, if there is any virtue and if there is anything praiseworthy—meditate on these things. The things which you learned and received and heard and saw in me, these do, and the God of peace will be with you.
(Philippians 4:8–9)

There's that peace again. Jesus promises us peace IF and it's a big IF. IF we do the things we've learned and received concerning Him, which implies we have to be spending time with Him. When we do spend time with Him and copy the things we observe, it will help us to meditate, think on, ponder and consider the things around us that are lovely, praiseworthy, virtuous, and true.

Jesus is known as the Word of God. John 14 tells us that the Word, Jesus became flesh and dwelt among us. The predicament is that although the Word has ascended into Heaven and has left us with wonderful words of life straight from the throne of grace, most Christians, unfortunately, don't read them. Barna Research Group in their 2017 Leading in Complexities Group said:

- 135 Million Americans are still favorable towards the Bible but many are distracted.

- Only 17% of Christians are engaged in the Bible

- Skeptics in our country have grown from being 10% of the population to 21%

The other challenge is that typically people are not avid readers. So not only are people not reading the Bible, they generally are not reading period. Now I, too, would not describe myself as an avid reader, which seems odd considering that I am an author and I have an online women's book club. But I do listen to audio books, and I listen to the Bible this way, too. Who cares how you get your time in with Jesus, just get it in. Your present and future depend on it. But all too frequently, believers tend to rely on others, mainly Pastors to teach us what the Bible says. This would be like me relying on eating a healthy meal only when my husband was inspired to cook. Let me tell you, I would starve! He might cook for me a handful of times a year—might.

But you say, "Oh, I go to church every week and my Pastor serves up a great spiritual meal." Well that's good. But not good enough. Try only eating once a week for only 90 minutes on a certain day and see what happens to your energy level, concentration, temperament, mood, and overall health. You might initially lose the extra weight you wanted, which might get you excited, but over time, you would become malnourished.

Malnourished Christians are surviving Christians, and Jesus intended for you to thrive. Feast on the Bread of Life, Jesus, every day. And when you do, thinking on thoughts that are lovely, just, pure, true and praiseworthy becomes easy. It becomes a part of your daily routine— your regular diet. And you know what they say: You are what you eat. But in this case you are what you think.

If all of us sent every thought that comes through our minds during the course of the day through the filter system described in Philippians 4:8, many thoughts that turn into doubt, fear or stress would immediately be dealt with. I want to challenge you. The next time a thought pops into your head that is less than lovely, say this aloud:

> "This thought of (fill in the blank) is not just, true, praiseworthy or pure so it is not allowed to stay in my mind. I have the mind of Christ. So my mind is controlled and calm."

Remember, you are what you eat. Or in this case, you are what you think. Think, meditate on, and say what you want, not what you don't want.

Chapter 9 | How Will Eliminating **Either/Or** Thoughts Affect My Life?

Our experiences in life are a direct result of our thinking and our perspective.

As he thinks in his heart so is he. (Proverbs 23:7a)

We can't always control what happens to us, but we can control how those things affect us. In life, there are always two lessons being taught:

1. What God wants us to walk away with.

2. What the enemy wants us to be bogged down with.

We get to choose, which messages we believe. The ones we embrace will determine our longevity and our destiny. By now you may have identified areas in your life that could use a thought-renewal overhaul. With those thoughts in mind take a few moments to jot down a response that counteracts the negative thought. For example:

> **Either/Or** thought: I can **Either** stay married and be miserable **Or** I can be single and alone.

> **Response**: God didn't bless me with a covenant marriage to be miserable. He created marriage and so He has all of the solutions my spouse and I need to succeed in marriage. I trust His wisdom and will humble myself if necessary in order to

experience God's best. I believe He will give us life strategies, and I am committed to making this relationship work by God's grace.

Make Your Confessions

It's your turn. Again, grab your notebook or journal and review your previous **Either/Or** thoughts and now write your responses to them. Once you have completed this exercise, reflect on how your life will be affected if you start thinking the healthier way. Will you have more joy, peace, and contentment? Will you obtain the boldness you need to step out into a new venture? Will you stress less? Will you become more financially secure? Will you enjoy the benefits of nurturing healthier, authentic relationships? I am confident that you can say "yes" to most, if not all, of these questions, and perhaps, you can think of even more benefits to getting rid of Either/Or thinking. You are an awesome child of God filled with amazing promise.

Chapter 10 | Action Steps

Saying your responses as a confession or affirmation is good, but don't stop there. Choose to study the Bible concerning the **Either/Or** thoughts you listed. Be led by the Holy Spirit to read other books on the subject. You can also attend conferences, classes, seminars, or groups. Educate yourself. You might be surprised to see how something that was once challenging for you may actually be tied to your purpose, gifts, increase, or future relationships. God can take a mess and make a masterpiece out of it if we let Him. Let Holy Spirit be your tour guide through life and teach you how to make a masterpiece out of your thoughts so you can see it show up in your life.

- Choose to study the Bible concerning the **Either/Or** thoughts you listed.

- Be led by the Holy Spirit to read other books on the subject.

- Educate yourself by attending conferences, classes, seminars, or groups.

You might be surprised to see how something that was once challenging for you may actually be tied to your purpose, gifts, increase, or future relationships. God can take a mess and make a masterpiece out of it if we let Him. Let Holy Spirit be your tour guide through life and teach you how to make a masterpiece out of your thoughts.

Book Review

Continue to review the steps necessary to identify and dismantle **Either/Or** thoughts:

- Understand that all thoughts do not come from you and God. Some are sent by the enemy to distract you from your purpose or get you to question your God-given identity.

- Pray, journal, ask God and others to help you identify some of your limiting mindsets.

- Once you identify them, write them down and write down an opposing statement.

- Say the opposite thoughts or statements aloud frequently enough that you begin to believe them.

- Find scriptures that support the positive thoughts and disagree with the negative ones.

- Surround yourself with the right people.

- Develop discriminating senses (choose your media outlets, entertainment, and close relationships wisely).

- Say what you want, not what you don't want. "Death and life are in the power of the tongue." (Prov. 18:21a).

Chapter 11: Final Thoughts

I hope you have found this book to be helpful to you in your quest of mind renewal. I would love to hear from you. Please visit my website at *www.EricaRenee.co.*

The one take-away I want you to have is this: God loves you. Yes, you! In spite of your flaws and circumstances and past, He loves you. He loves you so much that He sent His Son Jesus to die on a cross for you thousands of years before you were even born knowing that you might reject Him. He still thought you were worth the sacrifice and so do I. Please do me the honor of allowing me to walk you through what many call the sinner's prayer. I like to call it the salvation prayer.

But what does it say? "The word is near you, in your mouth and in your heart" (that is, the word of faith which we preach): that if you confess with your mouth the Lord Jesus and believe in your heart that God has raised Him from the dead, you will be saved. For with the heart one believes unto righteousness, and with the mouth confession is made unto salvation.
(Romans 10:8–10)

Based on this scripture, if you believe in your heart that Jesus died for your sin and you say that with your mouth, you are saved! Saved from what? From sin and its penalty. The wages of sin is death. Not just death physical, but emotional, spiritual, and any other way. Ultimately, sin separates us from God. Our source of life. And if you'd like to be reconnected to your life source, say this aloud:

"I believe that Jesus was sent by God to earth to die for my sins and that He rose from the dead. Thank you God for providing a savior for me so long ago. I receive Jesus today as my savior. Thank you for saving me from sin and its penalty. Thank you for wiping my slate clean and adopting me into your family. I am now a child of God. I am so grateful, and I trust you Holy Spirit to lead me as I develop into a mature believer."

Congratulations! If you prayed that prayer, you are now a born-again child who is adopted into God's family. Here are some scripture references to help you understand what has taken place:

Therefore, if anyone is in Christ, he is a new creation; old things have passed away; behold, all things have become new. [18] Now all things are of God, who has reconciled us to Himself through Jesus Christ, and has given us the ministry of reconciliation, [19] that is, that God was in Christ reconciling the world to Himself, not imputing their trespasses to them, and has committed to us the word of reconciliation. [20] Now then, we are ambassadors for Christ, as though God were pleading through us: we implore you on Christ's behalf, be reconciled to God. [21] For He made Him who knew no sin to be sin for us, that we might become the righteousness of God in Him.
(2 Corinthians 5:17–21)

For you did not receive the spirit of bondage again to fear, but you received the Spirit of adoption by whom we cry out, "Abba, Father." 16 The Spirit Himself bears witness with our spirit that we are children of God, 17 and if children, then heirs—heirs of God and joint heirs with Christ, if indeed we suffer with Him, that we may also be glorified together.
(Romans 8:15–17)

96

If you prayed this prayer for the first time or you prayed it again because you've strayed away from God but have returned, please let me know by visiting my website at *www.EricaRenee.co.* I would love to celebrate with you.

I also recommend that you get a Bible or Bible App that you will read or listen to and join a local church that will teach you the Bible and help you to grow in your Christian walk. God bless you!

About the Author

Erica Renée is a proud wife and mother of four beautiful children. She and her husband, Sean R. Moore, pastor a thriving church in Phoenix, AZ, Faith Christian Center. They met at Michigan State University, where she graduated with a BA in Communication. Erica is a licensed and ordained minister and has been a Christ follower since she was a young child.

Erica's teaching is packed with life-enhancing truths and delivered with humor and simplicity at church services, events, and conferences. She is the founder of the women's ministry, Woman2Woman and the W2W book club. Her goal is to empower women to be their best as she writes and speaks the truth in love. You can visit her website at *www.EricaRenee.co*. If you would like information regarding Woman2Woman, the book club, or Faith Christian Center, please visit www.fcc-phx.com.

Made in the USA
San Bernardino, CA
22 November 2017